Windows to the World: Literature in Christian Perspective

Windows to the World: Literature in Christian Perspective

Leland Ryken

Wipf and Stock Publishers
150 West Broadway • Eugene OR 97401
2000

Windows to the World: Literature in Christian Perspective

By Ryken, Leland
Copyright©2000 by Ryken, Leland

ISBN: 1-57910-340-5

Reprinted by *Wipf and Stock Publishers*
150 West Broadway • Eugene OR 97401

Previously Published by Word Publishign, 1990.

What Is Probe?

Probe Books are published by Probe Ministries, a nonprofit corporation whose mission is to reclaim the primacy of Christian thought and values in Western culture through media, education, and literature. In seeking to accomplish this mission, Probe provides perspective on the integration of the academic disciplines and historic Christianity. The members and associates of the Probe team are actively engaged in research as well as lecturing and interacting with students and faculty in thousands of university classrooms throughout the United States and Canada on topics and issues vital to the university student.

In addition, Probe acts as a clearing house, communicating the results of its research to the church and society.

Further information about Probe's materials and ministries may be obtained by writing to Probe Ministries International, P.O. Box 801046, Dallas, Texas 75204.

Other Books by Leland Ryken

The Apocalyptic Vision in "Paradise Lost"

The Christian Imagination (editor)

Contemporary Literary Theory: An Appraisal (co-editor)

Culture in Christian Perspective

Effective Bible Teaching (co-author)

How to Read the Bible as Literature

The Liberated Imagination: Thinking Christianly about the Arts

The Literature of the Bible

Milton and Scriptural Tradition (co-editor)

The New Testament in Literary Criticism (editor)

Triumphs of the Imagination

Words of Delight: A Literary Introduction to the Bible

Words of Life: A Literary Introduction to the New Testament

Work and Leisure in Christian Perspective

Worldly Saints: The Puritans as They Really Were

Contents

Acknowledgments

Appreciation is expressed to the following publishers for permission to use materials to which they hold copyright:

To Liveright Publishing Corporation for permission to reprint "in Just—" from *Tulips and Chimneys* by E. E. Cummings, used by permission of Liveright Publishing Corporation. Copyright 1923, 1925, and renewed 1951, 1953 by E. E. Cummings. Copyright © 1973, 1976 by the Trustees for the E. E. Cummings Trust. Copyright © 1973, 1976 by George James Firmage.

To Harvard University Press for permission to quote from poem #341 in *The Complete Poems of Emily Dickinson*, edited by Thomas H. Johnson. Reprinted by permission of the publishers and the Trustees of Amherst College from *The Poems of Emily Dickinson*, ed. Thomas H. Johnson (Cambridge, Mass.: Belknap Press), copyright © 1951, 1955, 1979, 1983 by the President and Fellows of Harvard College.

To Little, Brown and Company for permission to quote from poem #341 in *The Complete Poems of Emily Dickinson*, edited by Thomas H. Johnson. Copyright 1929 by Martha Dickinson Bianchi; copyright © renewed 1957 by Mary L. Hampson. By permission of Little, Brown and Company.

To Viking Penguin, Inc., for permission to quote part of "Araby" from *Dubliners* by James Joyce. Originally published by B. W. Huebsch

Preface

This is a book about literature. Its goal is to enhance your enjoyment and understanding of literature by uncovering some of the principles that underlie literature and its study. Ralph Waldo Emerson said that the purpose of principles is that they give us eyes to see something. This book will give you "eyes" with which to get the most out of your reading.

Current literary theory is preoccupied with the notion of "interpretive communities"—groups of readers who tend to assimilate literature in a common way because they share the same set of assumptions and interests. Christian readers are an interpretive community. They are not better readers of literature than other people, but they have their own agenda of interests, beliefs, and attitudes that they bring to the reading and study of literature. Like other readers, they read literature through their own "lens" and are sensitive to certain aspects of literature because they approach it with their own set of "antennae." This book is an attempt to make explicit what the interests of Christian readers are and how those presuppositions affect the reading and study of literature.

This book presupposes an interest in Christianity, but I have written it equally for Christians and non-Christians. Before writing the book, I listed the objections that I would bring to a book about literature that was written from a definite ideological bias (such as Marxism or feminism). I would expect such a book to treat only those aspects of literature that directly touch upon the writer's ideology. I would expect it to ignore matters of literary form and to treat literature as propaganda. I would expect the author to ignore the general interests of humanity and to disparage works of literature that did not conform to the writer's bias. These are my suspicions, and whenever they turn out to be wrong, I am particularly delighted by the writer's breadth of vision.

Aware of the dangers, I have tried my best to avoid them in this book. The resulting format is as follows. The first three-fourths of each chapter discuss a given literary topic as I think any good literary critic might wish it discussed. I then round off each chapter by fitting that data into a Christian framework. The fact that the Christian framework is provided after a given literary topic has been explored does not mean that it is "tacked on." It is purely an organizational strategy: before we can integrate Christianity with something else, we need to establish the thing *to which* we are relating Christianity. The Christian context at the end of the chapters is not like frosting on a cake but like a bookcase into which we place books: we must first assemble the books and then put them into the bookcase, and without the books the purpose of the bookcase is not apparent.

I hope that non-Christians will enjoy and benefit from listening in on this last part, in which I discuss matters from a Christian perspective. It goes without saying that Christian readers cannot afford to ignore the aspects of reading literature that they share with all readers.

The individual chapters of this book hang together as a coherent whole. No single chapter should be read in isolation from the others. Chapters on the content of literature need to be balanced by the chapter on literary form. My remarks on the role of the writer should not be considered without an awareness of what I say about the role of the reader in the next chapter. When I discuss morality as a criterion for judging literature in the last chapter, I do not intend this as the *only* aspect of literature that requires our attention. I offer this commonsensical advice because of a perverse tendency, especially among scholarly readers, to be preoccupied with what is being omitted at a given point in a book instead of waiting to see what a writer might have to say on that topic at another point in the book.

Book Abstract

In centuries when Western culture was dominated by the Judeo-Christian world view, few people questioned that literature should be produced and read within a Christian framework. As secularism gradually conquered the West, both the writing and study of literature became increasingly isolated from religious and moral concerns.

Sensing the gap between religion and literature, Christians began to regard literature as trivial or threatening to Christian standards. Detractors charged literature with being untruthful, immoral, and a waste of time. By contrast, humanistic enthusiasts for the arts made them a substitute religion for the Christian faith.

In this book the author carefully treads a middle path, affirming the value of reading literature while avoiding the excesses of either claiming too much for literature and ignoring all dangers or emphasizing all the negatives to the neglect of its benefits.

The author believes that literature, in its proper place, can be of great benefit to readers; it can give us windows to the world. Literature, like other arts, can allow us to travel through our imaginations unrestricted by time and space in order to observe, to learn, to be entertained. And, we can grow in the process, for imaginative literature, strange though it seems, excels at

15

helping us "see" the truth when it has eluded us before.

An examination of literature as recreation demonstrates that reading can be a wise and worthy use of leisure time. The author's discussion of persuasion leads us through some of the common techniques writers use to convince us of the rightness of their imaginary world. A related chapter explains how our responses as readers are a vital part of the reading process, without which the writer's work is incomplete.

The author reveals how reading is able to strengthen our faith as we learn to compare and contrast what we read with the biblical world view. Finally the author tackles the sometimes difficult subject of morality in literature. He argues that subject matter, in and of itself, is not an adequate basis for determining the morality of literature. More important, he says, may be the moral perspective of the literature in question or the effect of the literature on the reader.

chapter one

Why Literature Is Good for You

Literature is both useful and delightful. It is a form of knowledge and a type of entertainment. Literature can be defined as an interpretive presentation of human experience in an artistic form.

The Case Against Literature

"Why should I have to take a literature course? Literature doesn't tell me anything that a newspaper can't tell me."

"Reading novels is a waste of time. Novels aren't even factual."

"What can you do with a literature major?"

Have you ever heard questions like these? Of course you have. Everyone has. The criticisms leveled against literature through the centuries fall mainly into seven categories:

1. Literature does not communicate facts or useful information.

17

2. Literature teaches error.
3. Literature is merely pleasurable and entertaining and serves no useful purpose.
4. Literature is too emotional.
5. Literature is a waste of time.
6. Literature is fictional and therefore unrelated to life.
7. Literature is immoral.

These are important arguments and deserve to be taken seriously. It so happens that there are good answers to them. This entire book is an attempt to uncover those answers.

Defining Literature: The Voice of Human Experience

A good starting point is to define what literature is. Most obviously, literature is words or language. So is a newspaper, a biology book, and a speech. What makes literature different?

It is customary to distinguish the literary use of language from the expository use. Expository writing is language used to communicate information and facts. It is the kind of writing that is done in introductory college writing courses.

Here is an example of how expository writing might report the death of a young girl:

Lucy Brown, two-year-old daughter of Mr. and Mrs. Paul R. Brown of 1410 Evergreen Drive, passed away at the Good Samaritan Hospital last Tuesday, March 17. Death followed an attack of pneumonia. Interment was at Woodlawn Cemetery.

The main features of this account are that it contains the information or facts *about* the event and that it is objective. This is what the expository or practical use of language is best at. Notice, though, what *doesn't* get communicated: the "spirit" of the event, how the family and friends of the girl actually experienced the death, the subjective side of the experience.

Here is a second example of expository writing on the experience of death, an analysis of the effects of death by a psychologist:

The death of a friend or relative leads to some degree of resocialization; that is, it leads to some adjustment in one's *self*. There is a new relationship with the deceased now, one located primarily in the memory of past experiences . . . ; there are new feelings of grief and shock and loss that are slowly integrated into the self by the *I*.[1]

Observe how abstract the terminology is: "death," "resocialization," "feelings of grief and shock and loss." The writer is busy analyzing and labeling the experience. This is the customary type of knowledge that the sciences (including the social sciences) give us.

Compare the two expository passages on death to the following literary version of the same experience, part of a poem by the nineteenth-century American poet Emily Dickinson:

After great pain, a formal feeling comes—
The Nerves sit ceremonious, like Tombs. . . .

The Feet, mechanical, go round—
Of Ground, or Air, or Ought—
A Wooden way
Regardless grown,
A Quartz contentment, like a stone—

This is the Hour of Lead—
Remembered, if outlived,
As Freezing persons recollect the Snow—
First—Chill—then Stupor—then the letting go—

The first thing we notice about the poem is its concreteness, especially in the form of images of hardness ("tombs," "wooden," "quartz," "lead"). The poem appeals chiefly to our senses and imagination (the image-making capacity within us), whereas the expository accounts are slanted toward the abstract intellect.

The poem tells us both more and less than the newspaper report does. The newspaper account conveys much more information; its great virtue is the ability to give us the facts of the matter. The poem, however, communicates the spirit or atmosphere of the incident. It gives us a sense of the actual *experience* of the death as it affects the acquaintances of the deceased. The poem captures a common human response to death. It does so indirectly, by presenting images of hardness and numbness and loss of consciousness that we are meant to interpret as being *like* the impact of death. We should note, too, that the poem universalizes the experience; it will never go "out of date," whereas the newspaper account will.

Let's make another comparison between the expository and literary uses of language. A botanist studies a landscape and has this to say:

> Environment is highly complex and integrated. . . . The problem of measuring those physical conditions that really govern plant behavior is much more difficult than is commonly conceived. . . . The intensity of most factors varies with the hour, day, and season, and the rates of change, the durations of particular intensities. . . . The common practice of integrating measurements taken over a period of time as mean values may obscure very important time aspects of factor variation.[2]

This passage epitomizes the methods of the sciences. The sciences are preoccupied with measuring and quantifying reality. This is one way of "knowing" our world, but not the only way.

In contrast to the botanist's report of a landscape, here is what Mark Twain recorded:

> The dawn creeps in stealthily; the solid walls of black forest soften to gray, and vast stretches of the river open up and reveal themselves; the water is glass-smooth, gives off spectral wreaths of white mist; there is not the faintest breath of wind, nor stir of leaf; the tranquillity is profound and infinitely satisfying. . . . Well, that is all beautiful; soft and rich and beautiful; and when the sun gets well up, and distributes a pink flush here and a powder of gold yonder and a purple haze where it will yield the best effect, you grant that you have seen something that is worth remembering.[3]

Before noting how this passage differs from the previous one, we should note what they have in common: Mark Twain's description is as thoroughly rooted in the facts of reality as is the scientist's. But the approach of literature to those facts is far different. Mark Twain is obviously not interested in quantifying the landscape. Instead, he aims to convey the *quality* of the landscape. The literary description is also highly subjective; it interprets the meaning of the scene in terms of its tranquillity and beauty. And the passage is concrete and vivid rather than abstract and statistical.*

It would be wrong to conclude that the scientific account is a form of knowledge, while the literary description is not. They are both forms of knowledge. Science in times past has claimed an objectivity in knowledge (empiricism) which it in reality never possessed. Both literary and scientific knowledge entail a certain quality of subjectivity in theory and in practice. The kind of knowledge that literature imparts is an experiential knowledge, fully as important to human well-being as scientific knowledge. In the passage previously quoted, for example, we read Mark Twain's moving description of dawn's arrival on a river landscape. A moment's reflection on that passage easily convinces us of the value of experiential knowledge transferred through literature. In a discussion of poetry, Matthew Arnold, nineteenth-century English poet and critic, made a similar point—that is, literature can give us an enhanced knowledge of reality:

> The grand power of poetry is its interpretative power . . . , the power of so dealing with things as to awaken in us a wonderfully full, new, and intimate sense of them, and of our relations with them. When this sense is awakened in us, . . . we

*By concrete versus abstract I mean analogically that an abstract number like *8* means something *statistically*, but it is not as concrete a *picture* in our minds as the statement "eight apples," which draws a vivid imagining for us.

feel ourselves to be in contact with the essential nature of those objects, to be no longer bewildered and oppressed by them, but to have their secret, and to be in harmony with them.[4]

Literature, in other words, conveys a valuable form of human understanding and insight. It helps us begin to grasp the essential nature of reality, albeit a somewhat subjective grasp. Reading literature, therefore, yields a worthwhile form of knowledge, valuable even though different in quality from scientific knowledge.

Here is yet another comparison that will highlight the nature of literature. A young man once asked Jesus, "Who is my neighbor?" One way of answering the question would be to define "neighbor" and describe our duty to such a person, something like this: "Our neighbor is any person we encounter in need. Our duty to our neighbor is to go out of our way to meet the need."

Jesus did not choose the expository way of answering the question. Instead, He told a story, the parable of the Good Samaritan (Luke 10:29–37). The story itself is a literary "definition" of "neighbor." How does the literary definition differ from the expository one? It is concrete. It obeys the literary impulse to *show* rather than *tell* abstractly. It offers an *experience* of neighborliness, not a definition of it.

The fact that much expository writing makes some use of literary techniques (such as concrete imagery or story elements) should not be allowed to obscure the distinctiveness of the literary use of language. We should picture a continuum, with expository writing at one end and literature at the other. The presence of "mixed" writing does not invalidate the description of literature that I have provided.*

*The same point is made by John Reichert, *Making Sense of Literature* (Chicago: University of Chicago Press, 1977), who offers this list of qualities that we associate with literary texts (p. 169): "fictiveness; special care taken with form or with language; the use of concrete and sensuous detail; a

What is literature? Its subject is human experience. Its aim is to embody the very quality of life as we actually experience it. Literature is an *incarnation* of ideas or meanings, just as in Christian belief Jesus was the incarnation (enfleshment) of the invisible God in bodily human form. Literature does not primarily convey information *about* experience but actually *presents* the experience, as concretely and vividly as possible. Literature is like a book as compared with a book review, or like a picture rather than the written instructions in the directions for assembling an appliance.

Someone who made a survey of why college students read literature found that

**Literature: A
Window to
Reality**

> the students value literature as a means of enlarging their knowledge of the world, because through literature they acquire not so much additional *information* as additional *experience*. New understanding is conveyed to them dynamically and personally. Literature provides a *living-through*, not simply *knowledge about:* not the fact that lovers have died young and fair, but a living-through of *Romeo and Juliet;* not theories about Rome, but a living-through of the conflicts in *Julius Caesar* . . . .[5]

stress on unity and 'self-containedness'; emotiveness, perhaps, and entertainment value; or perhaps high seriousness and a special blending of the particular and the universal.'' For further examples of the distinctions I make between literary and expository uses of language, these sources will prove helpful: Laurence Perrine, *Sound and Sense: An Introduction to Poetry* (New York: Harcourt Brace Jovanovich, 1956, 1963, 1969, 1973), chap. 1; C. S. Lewis, ''The Language of Religion,'' in *Christian Reflections* (Grand Rapids: Eerdmans, 1967), pp. 129–41; Cleanth Brooks and Robert Penn Warren, *Understanding Poetry* (New York: Holt, Rinehart and Winston, 1938, 1950, 1960, 1976), chap. 1; William C. Handy, *Kant and the Southern New Critics* (Austin: University of Texas Press, 1963); Jurij Lotman, *The Structure of the Artistic Text*, trans. Ronald Vroon (Ann Arbor: University of Michigan Press, 1977).

A story or poem or play is a window or lens through which we look at experience and life. The following diagram illustrates what I mean:

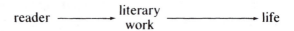

reader ⟶ literary work ⟶ life

As readers, we rivet our attention on the scenes and characters and events and images of a story or poem. But as we look *at* the work, we at the same time look *through* it to life and our own experiences.

As we read a poem or watch a movie, we stare at some aspect of human experience. While seeming to pay attention only to the immediate foreground details, we are actually looking at life in general. Someone has said that the writer's task "is to *stare*, to *look* at the created world, and to lure the rest of us into a similar act of contemplation."[6] The English novelist Joseph Conrad said something similar: "My task . . . is, by the power of the written word to make you hear, to make you feel—it is, before all, to make you *see*."[7]

What aspects of life do we look at when we read literature? While literature as a whole takes all of life as its subject, it is particularly adept at expressing certain aspects of life. One of these is the external world that we see and hear and smell and touch. Literature also has an unusual ability to capture the inner weather of human feelings and moods. The workings of the human psyche have been a frequent subject of literature. The moral world of good and evil, virtue and vice, is embodied in the world's literature, as is the supernatural world. There also is the world of social relationships and institutions, such as home and state.

However, *Time Magazine* and a psychology book may also deal with some of these subjects. How is literature different in its approach to them? There are three answers. I have already shown that whereas other disciplines tend to give the facts *about* a subject, the strategy of literature is to recreate the experience—to get inside the subject so we can "know" it experientially and concretely.

Another characteristic of literature is that it has a mysterious ability to capture what is enduring and universal in human experience. All of the concrete details of a story or poem are a net to capture something more general and universal. This does not mean that the concrete particulars are expendable. The approach of literature to the universal is always *through* the particular and concrete. We can sum up the matter by saying that *Newsweek* and a history book tell us what *happened,* whereas literature tells us what *happens.*

In the third place, literature not only presents human experience but offers an interpretation of it. In most cases literature deals with the same topics (nature, society, God, the individual) as other disciplines do. What distinguishes literature is that it looks at these things, not objectively, but as they are of concern and value *to people.*

Literature always filters reality through the consciousness of a valuing being. In the passage I quoted earlier from the botanist, we do not know how the scientist studying the landscape felt about it. He was too busy measuring it, and, besides, his aim was to be as objective as possible. By contrast, we *do* know how Mark Twain felt about the Mississippi River. A sociologist gives us statistics about crime, but Shakespeare's *Macbeth* makes us feel the horror and moral evil of crime.

We need both kinds of knowledge. We need the objective information that the sciences and "thought disciplines" can give us. But we also

The
Distinctiveness of
Literature

need to know about reality as perceived and experienced by people. To find the most reliable index to human values, fears, and longings, one should look at the arts, including literature.

Is literature useful? It is useful as long as it is important to know about human nature, human experience, human values, and human responses to the world.

The Values and Functions of Literature

Thus far I have tried to describe what literature *is*. The further question is, Of what *use* is literature? The values and functions of literature follow logically from what I have said literature is.

1. Understanding Human Experience

In the first place, literature is one of the leading ways in which the human race grapples with and interprets reality. The subject of literature is human experience. By staring at something closely, we ordinarily come to understand it better, especially if someone is present to point things out to us. This is one of the functions of literary writers. They take us by the hand and say, "Look." And as we look where they point, we discover and recover insights into the world and our experiences in it. By focusing our thought on a selected aspect of life, a work of literature clarifies our understanding of it.

2. Enlarging Our Being

Sometimes literature gives shape to experiences and viewpoints that we ourselves have not had. In such cases, literature enlarges us. As C. S. Lewis, the famous British literary scholar, Christian apologist, and beloved fantasy writer, expressed it,

We seek an enlargement of our being. We want to be more than ourselves. Each of us by nature sees the whole world from one point of view with a perspective and a selectiveness peculiar to himself. . . . We want to see with other eyes, to imagine with other imaginations, to feel with other hearts, as well as with our own. . . . We demand windows. . . . This, so far as I can see, is the specific value or good of literature. . . ; it admits us to experiences other than our own. . . . My own eyes are not enough for me, I will see through those of others.[8]

3. Giving Form to Our Own Experiences

At other times, literature embodies experiences that we, too, have had. In such instances, literature gives form to our own feelings and experiences and beliefs. What lies in chaotic or inarticulate form within us, perhaps just below the level of consciousness, is projected onto the scenes and events and characters in a work of literature. The writer is our representative, saying what we want said, only saying it better, perhaps, than we can.

Literature serves this function whenever it leads us to say, "How like real life!" If Socrates was right when he said that the unexamined life is not worth living, literature carries it one step further and adds that the unexpressed life is also incomplete. Ralph Waldo Emerson, the transcendentalist poet and essayist, said it well:

> The poet is representative. . . . All men live by truth and stand in need of expression. . . . Notwithstanding this necessity. . . , adequate expression is rare. . . . Poets are natural sayers, sent into the world to the end of expression.[9]

Literature gives shape and expression to our own experiences, insights, and values.

4. Heightened Awareness

In view of what I have been saying, we would do well to look upon literature as a chief means (though not the only means) by which we can *heighten our awareness*—awareness of ourselves, of the world, of other people, of God. As we read and think about a story or poem, we are made aware of some facet of human experience.

This is a more modest defense of literature than we often hear. It strikes me as untrue that literature regularly gives brand new insights that we cannot get from anywhere else. But I am continually impressed by how consistently literature gives me a heightened awareness of something. I do not need Mark Twain to tell me that nature is beautiful. I already know that. But I am enriched by his making me *aware* of the manifold beauties of nature.

Literature sensitizes us to the world around us and within us. The English Romantic poet Samuel Taylor Coleridge wrote, "Who has not a thousand times seen snow fall on water? Who has not watched it with a new feeling from the time he has read Burns' [description of it]?"[10] Notice the key phrase: "with a new feeling." The writer's task is one of revelation—of removing the obstacles to our awareness of life.

In addition to fostering our *self*-awareness, literature gets us beyond ourselves and heightens our awareness of other people. Because the subject of literature is human experience, reading literature awakens us to the experiences of people around us. It makes us sensitive to human needs. It is one of the ways by which we can have our sense of compassion enlarged, partly because literature (especially modern literature) leads us to encounter types of experience that we would otherwise avoid. Literature makes us participants in the joys and sorrows, the agony and the ecstasy, of the human race.

5. A Catalyst to Thinking

Literature also stimulates our thinking about the great issues and ideas of life. A story or poem embodies a perspective on life. Literature as a whole presents the world views by which people have lived and continue to live. This, too, is a type of knowledge worth having. Surely one of the reasons why (according to a Gallup poll) 58 percent of Americans have never finished reading a book is that reading literature requires a person to think.[11] Great literature is the enemy of the idle mind.

6. Literature As Recreation and Entertainment

The values of literature that I have discussed thus far have all had to do with the usefulness of literature. But there is another function of literature that is equally important. Literature is fun. It provides the materials and occasion for recreation or enjoyment. C. S. Lewis claimed that "a great deal (not all) of our literature was made to be read lightly, for entertainment. If we do not read it, in a sense, 'for fun' . . . we are not using it as it was meant to be used."[12] Literature carries its own reward as a leisure time pursuit.

Tennis and jogging are also leisure pursuits. What does literature have to commend it over other forms of recreation? It makes us think. It awakens our minds and imaginations and emotions. Because of its subject matter, it puts us in touch with human experience and human values. We need sports to be physically fit, but we also need forms of recreation that engage our minds and imaginations, forms that humanize us.

Levels of Truth in Literature

Does literature tell the truth? That question sooner or later comes up in discussions about the value and function of literature. The answer depends on what we mean by "truth." It is easy to claim either too much or too little for the truthfulness of literature. We need to discern three levels of truth in literature.

1. Truth About Human Values

At the simplest and most general level, literature as a whole puts us in touch with *human values.* Regardless of what writers say about *God* or *nature,* for example, simply by what they choose to write about, they tell us the truth about what is *important* in human experience. If you want to know the truth about rock-bottom human nature—about what people *need* and *value* most—literature is probably your best source.

2. *Truthfulness to Reality and Human Experience*

A second level of truth in literature is truthfulness to the way things are in the world. I have said that the subject of literature is human experience. The traditional metaphor is that literature holds the mirror up to life. Whenever literature accurately captures the nature of human experience, it can be said to be true. We are obviously talking now about *the reality principle*. In this instance "truth" means truthfulness to reality, or *representational truth*. We have all read or viewed works of literature that struck us as far-fetched or implausible, *not* true to the way things are. But generally speaking, writers of literature are sensitive observers of reality, and most literature is, accordingly, true at this level.

3. *The Level of Ideas and Philosophy of Life*

In addition to presenting human experience, literature gives an *interpretation* of it. Literature gives us reality as filtered through the writer's bias. It is an implied comment about the experiences portrayed in the work. From any major work of literature, we can deduce one or more generalizations (called "themes") about life.

The range of viewpoints that we find in literature at this level is as varied and contradictory as we find in society at large. The claims that we can make for the truthfulness of literature at this level are much more limited than at the previous two levels. Writers of literature contradict each other and cannot all be telling us the truth. A pantheistic poet like Walt Whitman, a naturalistic writer like Thomas Hardy, and a Christian nature poet like Gerard Manley Hopkins cannot all be telling us the truth about nature. At the level of philosophic or moral viewpoint, therefore, we can never make a blanket statement that literature tells the truth.

For a provocative summary of the things that literature can do for us, the following quotation will repay careful attention:

Summary of the Functions of Literature

It presents material for the judgment of life and its phenomena; and along with this material it offers judgments on the material. It makes the reader more intensely conscious of the problems of life, of the predicaments of people, the possibilities and the limitations in living, the diversities in human experience, and some of the meanings, potential and actual, in this human experience. It makes value judgments on conditions, actions, thoughts, situations, environments, hopes, despairs, ideals, dreams, and fantasies. It provides its audience with additional equipment in proceeding with their own lives, and in the outward extension of their interests. It points their emotions, their impulses, their wishes, and their thoughts toward or away from certain goals. It creates, in an ideal and formal sense, the consciousness of an epoch, and is thus one of the instruments that work toward moulding and remoulding the human consciousness.[13]

You may have noticed how often the word *human* has come up in the preceding discussion. As I now slant the topic to the Christian element in society, I could well entitle my remarks "Welcome to the Human Race." Christians have no less responsibility, probably more, to be aware of what it means to be human than others have.

Why Christians Need Literature

This applies first to Christians as individuals. Self-knowledge is as important to Christians as anyone else. In reading literature, we see ourselves. Our responses to what we read say a lot about our own attitudes. In reading literature, we face what is best and worst in ourselves, what is hidden and repressed as well as what we are conscious of.

According to Christianity, *people matter.*
They have value because God made them and
redeemed them. God even took on human form.
To realize our full humanity is not frivolous.
Some forms of Christianity become so "other-
worldly" that they have an unbiblical scorn for
what is human rather than divine, and earthly
rather than heavenly. Literature *can be* a helpful
corrective. One of the most prevalent failures of
sermons and Bible studies and Sunday school
classes is that they are out of touch with real life
and human attitudes. Reading is one of the
ways, though not the only way, to stay in touch
with humanity.

There is also a social or moral dimension to
the Christian's immersion in human experience.
Christians feel both a humanitarian and evangel-
istic responsibility toward their society. They
are convinced that it is not enough to leave the
human race where it is. In order to discharge
that responsibility, they need to understand the
nature and needs of people. Literature and the
arts are perhaps the most accurate record that
we have of human needs, longings, and values.

Christians are usually a minority within their
culture. They are subject to all the tendencies of
other minorities: a sense of alienation from
culture as a whole, an in-group mentality and
vocabulary, an inclination to concentrate on
their distinctives and slight what they have in
common with all people simply by virtue of
being human, a "we-they" outlook on the
world. Reading literature is one good way to
counteract these tendencies. Literature belongs
to the whole human race. It binds people
together and overrides barriers as few other
things do.

There is, finally, a reason why Christians
should value literature that others may lack. It is
that the Bible is in large part literary in nature.
The Bible is a book for all seasons and contains
every type of writing, but more often than not it
follows the literary principles that I have noted

in this chapter. It tends to be concrete and experiential. It relies chiefly on literary forms (story, poetry, visions, letters). The one thing that the Bible is *not* is what Christians too often picture it as being—a theological outline with proof texts. Because the Bible communicates truth by literary means, no Christian can say that literature is unimportant.

Christians need literature, but the Christian faith also acts as a curb against excessive claims that have been made for literature. For nearly two centuries now, many secular writers and enthusiasts for literature have made literature and the imagination their *religion*. About a century ago English poet and critic Matthew Arnold pictured literature as replacing Christianity as the consolation to which people should turn; he wrote, ''More and more mankind will discover that we have to turn to poetry to interpret life for us, to console us, to sustain us. . . . Most of what now passes with us for religion and philosophy will be replaced by poetry.''[14] It is important for Christians to know about this trend so they will recognize exaggerated claims for literature when they encounter them. It is a very prevalent viewpoint and includes much of the ''religious'' or ''Christian'' approach to literature.

In commenting on the advantages of Christianity for a writer, Chad Walsh, a contemporary poet, says the Christian writer is saved from the romantic tendency toward idolatry: ''Art is not religion. . . . There is wisdom and illumination but not salvation in a sonnet.''[15] This is similar to C. S. Lewis's oft-quoted opinion that

The Christian will take literature a little less seriously than the cultured Pagan. . . . The unbeliever is always apt to make a kind of religion of his aesthetic experiences. . . . But the Christian knows from the outset that the salvation of a single soul is more important than the production and preservation of all the epics and tragedies in the world.[16]

SUMMARY

Literature is life. If you want to know what, deep down, people feel and experience, you can do no better than read the stories and poems of the human race. Writers of literature have the gift of observing and then expressing in words the essential experiences of people.

The rewards of reading literature are significant. Literature helps to humanize us. It expands our range of experiences. It fosters awareness of ourselves and the world. It enlarges our compassion for people. It awakens our imaginations. It expresses our feelings and insights about God, nature, and life. It enlivens our sense of beauty. And it is a constructive form of entertainment.

Christians should neither undervalue nor overvalue literature. It is not the ultimate source of truth. But it clarifies the human situation to which the Christian faith speaks. It does not replace the need for the facts that science and economics and history give us. But it gives us an experiential knowledge of life that we need just as much as those facts.

Literature does not always lead us to the City of God. But it makes our sojourn on earth much more a thing of beauty and joy and insight and humanity.

chapter two

Imagination: The "Lie" That Tells the Truth

Disciplines like biology, sociology, and psychology all have their own way of describing and organizing the world. So do the arts. Their way of seeing and arranging reality is through the imagination. The imagination transforms the materials of real life in such a way that, although not literal or factual, it allows us to see the truth.

"My love is like a red, red rose."

"I have measured out my life with coffee spoons."

"And they lived happily ever after."

It is obvious that writers of imaginative literature speak a language all their own. To read a work of literature is to enter a whole "world" of the imagination, a world that has its own rules and procedures.

Imagination: The "Language" of the Arts

35

The most obvious fact that we notice about the world of the imagination is that it differs from the physical world in which we live. It is not a literal, tangible world. For one thing, it exists only inside our heads. Studying literature is not done with a telescope, microscope, slide rule, or test tube

I am going to describe in this chapter some of the leading features of the artistic imagination. I will include music and the visual arts as well as literature, because what all the arts have in common is that they use the imagination as their way of expressing truth. Putting literature alongside music and the visual arts will clarify things greatly.

My main point is well summarized by a comment made by Picasso, the Spanish painter and sculptor. Picasso once stated that "art is a lie that makes us realize truth."[17] We need to do justice to both halves of that statement. On the one hand, the world that the imagination gives us is filled with things that are not literally or factually true. Yet this "lie" tells us much that is true and that cannot be adequately expressed in any other way.

The Concreteness of the Imagination

The first thing that we can say about the world of the imagination is that it tends to be a concrete sensory world. Look closely at the word *imagination*. It is built around the idea of *image*. Dorothy Sayers, British writer and translator of *The Divine Comedy*, described the nature of a work of art this way: "Suppose, having rejected the words 'copy,' 'imitation' and 'representation' as inadequate, we substitute the word 'image' and say that what the artist is doing is *to image forth* something or the other."[18]

A little reflection will show that this is right. All of the arts feed upon the physical world around us, including, of course, the human world. The visual arts work with very tangible materials to produce images that we experience with our eyes. The musician uses physical objects to produce sounds, and in the process often touches powerfully on the world of human emotions. The storyteller and dramatist write about something as actual as people in physical settings doing physical acts. And poets fill their poems with images of physical reality. It is no wonder that Northrop Frye, one of the world's leading literary critics, can write in his book *The Educated Imagination*, "Literature's world is a concrete human world of immediate experience. The poet uses images and objects and sensations much more than he uses abstract ideas; the novelist is concerned with telling stories, not with working out arguments."[19]

Now if the world of the imagination is as concrete as all this, how can I call it a "lie"? Let's explore the matter a little further.

For one thing, the arts rearrange physical reality and do not give it to us in exactly the same form that we find in actual life. Looking at a real scene is different from looking at a painting of the scene. The colors and lines and materials and dimensions of a painting are not those of nature. Painters do not, and cannot, exactly reproduce external appearances. Moreover, many of them deliberately distort physical reality. Even photography alters reality. And as for music, it gives us combinations of sounds that are not present in nature.

Furthermore, even when the imagination is concrete, it is usually using the concretion to say something else by a process of indirection. Consider, for example, Emily Dickinson's poem on death quoted earlier (page 19). It is filled with concrete images naming things we can touch: wood, stone, lead, snow. But the poem is not *about* these things. It is about the effect of death on a grieving person.

Or consider some examples from *The Divine Comedy* by Dante, the early fourteenth-century Italian poet. In this masterpiece of imaginative expression, the author tells the story of a person (Dante himself) who took a fictional journey through hell. In his account, Dante portrays various sins in physical terms. When the pilgrim comes to the place of the lustful, for example, he hears a howling wind and sees shades being blown everywhere. The picture is utterly concrete, but is literally a "lie." Lust is not really a wind that never ceases blowing. The truth of this "lie," however, is obvious: lust can grab control of a person the way wind swirls around and blows things before it.

When Dante comes to "the circle of the gluttons," he sees a scene that resembles a gigantic garbage pit on a snowy winter afternoon. It captures the nature of the sin of gluttony, but gluttony is not literally a garbage dump. Again, the unnaturalness of suicide is pictured as a sinister forest that is filled with dead and deformed trees. Now suicide is not really a forest. What Dante has done is what writers and other artists often do—that is, project (symbolically through the imagination) one thing as being, or representing, something else. Here Dante pictures moral and spiritual states as physical landscapes.

So for all its concreteness and reality, the world of the imagination is, at the literal level, false. The imagination gives us a barrage of concrete images and sensations, only to insist that they really mean something else. Robert Frost, the contemporary American poet, defined poetry as the attempt "to say one thing in terms of another."[20]

The Imaginary or Fictional Element in Imagination

Look at the word *imagination* again. It at once suggests the word *imagine*, thereby hinting at the fictional and fantastic nature of the arts. To imagine means to call into being something that does not actually exist. Artists have never felt obliged to limit their products to what exists in empirical reality.

This is perhaps most easily seen in literature. Stop to consider some of the fantastic things that poets and storytellers ask us to pretend. Poets expect us to believe (for the moment) that humans can go around speaking in rhyme and regular meter. The love poet praises his or her beloved as ideally beautiful and virtuous, one of a kind.

Storytellers sometimes create weird creatures like orcs and hobbits and talking animals (see, for example, J. R. R. Tolkien's work *The Lord of the Rings*). And even if they are realists, they fill their stories with things that do not literally happen in real life. For example, in stories we are always allowed to see the motivations of the characters that are portrayed, even though in real life motives often remain hidden. Storytellers are addicted to a narrative convention known as poetic justice, a situation in which good characters are rewarded and bad ones punished, even though we know that such justice is all too often lacking in real life.

Literary tragedy, so often praised for "telling it like it is," does not portray catastrophe as we experience it in real life. It omits, in the words of C. S. Lewis, "the clumsy and apparently meaningless bludgeoning of much real misfortune and the prosaic littlenesses which usually rob real sorrows of their dignity" and presents instead suffering "that is always significant and sublime."[21]

Every library's huge section that is called "fiction" is a reminder of how thoroughly much of the world's literature is made up, imagined, pretended. What is not so apparent is how thoroughly poetry, by which I mean *figures of speech*, likewise is fictional rather than factual. Someone has said that "over every poem which looks like a poem is a sign which reads . . .: fictitious."[22]

Consider, for example, the following poem by William Blake, the English poet and mystic. A kind of British folk hymn, it is more famous in

England than in the United States. For many Americans their first exposure to it came when they viewed the funeral service at the end of the movie *Chariots of Fire:*

And did those feet in ancient time
Walk upon England's mountains green?
And was the holy Lamb of God
On England's pleasant pastures seen?

And did the Countenance Divine
Shine forth upon our clouded hills?
And was Jerusalem builded here,
Among these dark Satanic Mills?

Bring me my Bow of burning gold:
Bring me my Arrows of desire:
Bring me my Spear: O clouds unfold!
Bring me my Chariot of fire!

I will not cease from Mental Fight,
Nor shall my Sword sleep in my hand,
Till we have built Jerusalem
In England's green and pleasant Land.

This poem portrays a specific British landscape, that of Glastonbury, located about a dozen miles from the sea. The sea once reached to Glastonbury, and according to a legend of the Middle Ages, Jesus at the age of twelve accompanied His uncle, Joseph of Arimathaea, a shipman, to the island that is today Glastonbury Tor ("Hill"). The legend also claimed that Jesus returned to the island sometime before His public ministry and built a little wattle hut thatched with reeds there. He stayed for a year or more, preparing for His great mission and planning the new age, which Blake in the poem calls "Jerusalem," based on the imagery of the New Testament Book of Revelation.

With this as background, look at the series of questions with which the poem begins. The literal, factual answer to these questions is "no." These things did not literally happen. But in making the point that Christian values should be a reality in contemporary society, the imagination is not obliged to stick to the facts.

And what about the poet's weapons in the third stanza? A bow of burning gold? Arrows of desire? A chariot of fire? Don't look for them at your local sporting goods store or used chariot dealer. You will, incidentally, find them in the Old Testament books of Isaiah and Jeremiah. And as for the poet's claim that he will not cease from mental fight till he has built Jerusalem in England's green and pleasant land, you will look in vain for the city of Jerusalem anywhere on the island of Britain.

What does the imagination do? It imagines. It makes things up. It tells us a lot that we know is not literally true. The contemporary Russian novelist Vladimir Nabokov has said, "Literature was born not on the day when a boy crying wolf, wolf came running . . . with a big gray wolf at his heels: literature was born on the day when a boy came crying wolf, wolf and there was no wolf behind him."[23]

A Heightened View of Reality

What else do the arts do that will support Picasso's description of them as a "lie"? They heighten reality beyond what we find in real life. Music, for example, heightens our feelings of love or exultation or gloom. And what about painting? It can even give us a heightened or concentrated perception of a side of beef, as in Rembrandt's painting entitled "Side of Beef Hanging in a Butcher Shop." The distortions or omissions or juxtapositions in paintings usually serve the function of highlighting the things or experience being portrayed. No doubt you have stood before a statue that is obviously larger than the person represented was or is in real life.

Such heightening is equally true of literature. The characters we meet in stories are more beautiful or more ugly, more heroic or more villainous, more vicious or more virtuous, than what we ordinarily find in real life. Love poetry is filled with ideally beautiful women and ideally ardent lovers. When, in real life, do falling in love and getting married result in people "living happily ever after"?

Even when literature does not exaggerate, it simplifies reality, and once again the subject is heightened in our awareness. Literature is never a journalistic reportage of everything that happens. It is not a recording of the mere flow of human experience. Instead, a writer distills from human experience what fits the pattern and theme of a story or poem. A love poet distills the beauty and attractiveness of the beloved. Modern novelists like Ernest Hemingway and William Faulkner distill the misery and cruelty and apparent meaninglessness of life, without worrying about a whole other side of life that we know also exists. By this process of selectivity, the imagination silhouettes a given subject with clarity.

The "One Story"
of Literature

Another general feature of the imagination is that it gives us a strongly unified world. In literature, especially, we continually encounter the same character types, plot motifs, and images. These recurrent images are called "archetypes." They are the basic building blocks of the literary imagination.

All of the persons, events, and images of literature make up a single composite story. This story is called the "monomyth" because it is the "one story" of literature.

The *monomyth* is shaped like a circle and has four separate phases. As such, it corresponds to some familiar cycles of human experience. The cycle of the year, for example, consists of the sequence of summer–fall–winter–spring. A day moves through a cycle consisting of sunrise–zenith–sunset–darkness. A person's life passes from birth to adulthood to decline and finally to death. The monomyth, too, is a cycle having four phases.

We can picture the "one story" of literature as in figure 1:

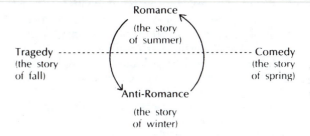

Romance (which Northrop Frye calls "the story of summer") pictures idealized human experience and is a wish-fulfillment dream of complete happiness. Its opposite, *anti-romance* ("the story of winter"), portrays unideal experience and is an anxiety dream of total bondage and frustration. *Tragedy* ("the story of fall") narrates a fall downward from bliss to catastrophe, and *comedy* ("the story of spring") narrates a rise from bondage to happiness and freedom. These are the four kinds of story or poem material, and together they make up the composite story of literature.

The monomyth is the most general or universal pattern to be found in literature. The circular pattern of the monomyth takes a number of specific forms, including the following:

1. *The quest,* in which the hero leaves the security of his home, undertakes an ordeal that tests his powers and temporarily defeats him, overcomes the obstacles, and either returns home in triumph or achieves a new state of bliss (which still constitutes a return to the initial state). Like the monomyth, the quest is circular in structure, its phases being separation, transformation through ordeal, and return.

2. *The death-rebirth motif,* in which a hero endures death or danger and returns to life or security.
3. *The initiation,* in which the hero is thrust out of an existing, usually ideal, situation and undergoes a series of ordeals as he or she passes from ignorance and immaturity to social or spiritual adulthood.
4. The *journey,* in which the hero passes through threats that test him and lead to his character development.
5. *Tragedy,* or its more specific form of the fall from innocence.
6. *Comedy,* a U-shaped story that begins in prosperity, descends into tragedy, but rises to a happy ending as obstacles to success are overcome.
7. *Crime and punishment,* in which the order of society is destroyed and the criminal undergoes punishment as social order is reestablished.
8. *The temptation motif,* in which an innocent person becomes the victim of an evil tempter or temptress.
9. *The rescue motif* (or the chase and rescue motif), in which characters undergo dire threat and then are rescued.
10. *The Cinderella or rags-to-riches pattern,* in which a character overcomes the obstacles of ostracism and poverty.
11. *The scapegoat motif,* in which a character with whom the welfare of society is identified must die for the sins of the people before prosperity can return to society.

These eleven plot motifs are, each in its own way, reenactments of the circular monomyth that encompasses all of literature. They are the most frequent ways in which the imagination organizes reality.

These same patterns are present in actual life, but not in the same concentrated way as we find them in literature. In daily living, for example, we rarely look at our own lives or the lives of others and fit them into the pattern of the quest toward a goal. But the moment we begin to read the stories of Abraham, Odysseus, Aeneas, the Joad family, or Frodo, we see the *quest motif* as the organizing pattern of the hero's life. When a young person takes a camping trip or goes off to college or begins a new job, we are only vaguely aware of the *initiation pattern,* but when we read the stories of Joseph, Telemachos, Candide, or Huckleberry Finn, we are fully aware that the protagonist is undergoing an initiation into the adult world. The landscapes that we encounter in real life are full of unorganized details, but the landscapes of literature have an easily discernible meaning—they are either the earthly paradise or the sinister forest or the wasteland or the idealized green world of pastoral.

The imagination rearranges the materials of real life. In doing so, it imposes a pattern or order on experience that differs from the random and disorganized details that make up our daily existence. Every work of literature that you will ever read can be plotted somewhere on the monomyth, but not every event in real life can be put there with the same ease.

There is one more thing to note about the archetypes that make up the world of the imagination. It is easy to arrange virtually all of the archetypal images of literature into two columns, one desirable, the other undesirable. The imagination is dualistic or dialectical (made up of opposites) when it arranges reality.

The best way to show the dualistic structure of literature is to list the archetypal images and character types that comprise it. See the following chart.

The Dualistic Nature of the Imagination

Category of Experience	The Archetypes of Ideal Experience	The Archetypes of Unideal Experience
The supernatural	Any beneficent deity; angels; the heavenly society.	Demons (including Satan), or malicious deities; hobgoblins, ogres; blind fate.
Human characters	The hero or heroine; the good mother or father; the innocent child; the benevolent king or ruler; the wiseman; the shepherd.	The villain; the tempter or temptress; the harlot (prostitute); the witch; the idiot; the taskmaster or tyrant; the wicked father or stepmother; the malicious parent; the outcast or wanderer; the traitor; the malicious giant; the shrewish or domineering woman; the sluggard or lazy person; any "blocking character" standing in the way of happiness; the churl or refuser of festivities.
Human relationships	The community or city; images of symposium, communion, order, unity, friendship, love; the wedding or marriage; the feast, meal, or supper; the family; freedom.	Tyranny or anarchy; isolation among people; images of torture, mutilation (the stocks, cross, stake, gallows, scaffold), slavery or bondage; images of war, riot, feud, or family discord.
Clothing	Any stately garment that symbolizes legitimate position or success; festal garments such as wedding clothes; fine clothing given as gifts of hospitality; white or light-colored clothing; clothing of adornment (such as jewels); protective clothing, such as a warrior's armor.	Ill-fitting garments (often symbolic of a position that is usurped and not held legitimately); garments symbolizing mourning (the shroud, dark mourning garments, sackcloth, mourning bands); dark clothes; tattered, dirty, or coarse clothing; any clothing that suggests poverty or bondage; a conspicuous excess of clothing (the overdressed person).
The human body	Images of health, strength, vitality, potency; feats of strength and dexterity; images of sleep and rest; wish-fulfillment dreams; birth.	Images of disease, deformity, barrenness, injury, or mutilation; sleeplessness or nightmare, often related to guilt of conscience; death.

Category of Experience	The Archetypes of Ideal Experience	The Archetypes of Unideal Experience
Food	Staples, such as bread, milk, and meat; luxuries, such as wine and honey; the harvest.	Hunger, drought, starvation, cannibalism; poison or magic potions.
Animals	A community of domesticated animals, usually a flock of sheep; a lamb; a gentle bird, often a dove; a faithful domesticated animal, such as a dog; a group of singing birds; the beneficent talking animals of folktales; animals or birds noted for their strength, such as the lion or eagle.	Monsters or beasts of prey; the wolf (enemy of sheep), the tiger, the dragon, the vulture, the cold and earthbound snake, the owl (associated with darkness), the hawk; any wild animal harmful to people; the scapegoat.
Landscape	A garden, grove, or park; the mountaintop or hill; the fertile and secure valley; pastoral settings or farms; the pathway.	The sinister or dark forest, often enchanted and in control of demonic forces; the heath or wilderness or wasteland, an area that is always barren and may be either a tropical place of intense heat or a place of ice and intense cold; the dark and dangerous valley; the underground cave or tomb; the graveyard; the labyrinth.
Plants	Green grass; the rose; the vineyard; the tree of life; the lily; evergreen plants (symbolic of immortality); herbs or plants of healing.	The thorn or thistle; weeds; dead or dying plants; the willow tree (symbolic of mourning).
Buildings	The city or palace or castle; the temple or church; the house or home; the tower of contemplation; the capital city, symbol of the nation; the rustic cottage.	The prison or dungeon; the wicked city of violence, sexual perversion, and crime; the tower of imprisonment or wicked aspiration (the tower of Babel).
The inorganic world	Images of jewels and precious stones, often glowing and fiery; fire and brilliant light; burning that purifies and refines; rocks of refuge.	The inorganic world in its unworked form of deserts, rocks, and wilderness; dry dust or ashes; fire that destroys and tortures instead of purifying; rust and decay.

Category of Experience	The Archetypes of Ideal Experience	The Archetypes of Unideal Experience
Water	A river or stream; a spring or fountain of water; showers of rain; dew; flowing water of any type; tranquil pools in a formal garden.	The sea and all that it contains (sea beasts and water monsters); stagnant pools.
Forces of nature	The breeze or wind; the spring and summer seasons; calm after storm; the sun or the lesser light of the moon and stars; light, sunrise, day.	The storm or tempest; the autumn and winter seasons; sunset, darkness, night.
Sounds	Musical harmony; singing; laughter.	Discordant sounds, cacophony, weeping, wailing.
Direction and motion	Images of ascent, rising, height (especially the mountaintop and tower), motion (as opposed to stagnation).	Images of descent, lowness, stagnation or immobility, suffocation, confinement.

In real life, things do not automatically fall into this dualistic pattern. Once again we see that the imagination, even when it takes its materials from the real world, transforms those materials into its own distinctive pattern. Notice, too, that virtually all of these archetypes are concrete in nature. Once again we can see the inclination of the imagination to formulate reality in concrete rather than abstract terms.*

*For more information on how archetypes work and why they affect us so powerfully, the following sources will prove helpful: Shirley Park Lowry, *Familiar Mysteries: The Truth in Myth* (New York: Oxford University Press, 1982); John B. Vickery, ed., *Myth and Literature: Contemporary Theory and Practice* (Lincoln: University of Nebraska Press, 1966); Northrop Frye, *Anatomy of Criticism* (Princeton: Princeton University Press, 1957), especially pp. 131–239; Leland Ryken, *Triumphs of the Imagination: Literature in Christian Perspective* (Downers Grove: InterVarsity Press, 1979), pp. 75–98 and 211–17. Most impressive of all is the large number of literature anthologies in recent years that are organized around archetypes instead of chronologically.

Other points might be added to this list of ways in which the imagination "falsifies" reality, but these are the most important. The imagination is a realm of concrete sensations and images that only partly resemble those in the real world and which, more often than not, are intended to represent something else that they literally are not. The imagination is always busy making things up, playing the game of "let's pretend," presenting as real, things that exist only in the imagination. The imagination heightens whatever it touches, either by exaggerating or simplifying or silhouetting a subject with striking clarity. The world of the imagination is organized as a single composite story and as a vast structure of opposites.

In case my emphasis on the way in which the imagination refashions external reality makes you begin to suspect it, let me add that even the factual disciplines rearrange life in this way. What a scientist sees under a microscope is not what we see around us. The facts in a psychological profile are not a complete account of the person sitting in front of us. The generalizations made in a history book are usually different from the immediate events that happened to a person living in a given age.

**Summary:
Imagination As a
"Lie"**

Before I attempt to make the case that the imagination's "lie" tells the truth, let me pause to notice that this world of the imagination has some other things that commend it, quite apart from its ability to embody truth. In a culture where fact rules, especially economic fact, and where the computer is often treated as the ultimate authority, it is refreshing to come upon something that does not defer to the fact. I am inclined to think that in our present cultural climate anything that resists quantifying and statistical tabulation might be, indeed, a welcome phenomenon.

The distortions that the arts make when they

**The Arresting
Strangeness of
the Imagination**

rearrange reality have another quality that commends them. It is the quality that J. R. R. Tolkien, author of *The Lord of the Rings* and other modern fantasy, ascribes to fairy tales, namely, "arresting strangeness"—strangeness that captures our attention. By giving us a version of reality that differs from what we normally perceive, the imagination compels our attention, making us take note of something that ordinarily escapes our notice. It "defamiliarizes" experience.*

Nor should we overlook the sheer delight that the imagined world of the arts gives to the human race. We can see evidence of people's affectionate addiction to stories and songs (poems, in other words) every day.

When the imagination works its magical transformation on reality, when it formulates its "lie" on canvas or in words or with music, the world takes note, unless other cultural forces have conditioned it not to. Now if these inherent advantages could be harnessed in the service of truth, we would have an ultimate medium. What if the intriguing "lie" of the imagination turns out to be the truth? Is it possible? It is.

In fact, everyone uses such "lies" in ordinary speech. We speak of the sun "rising" and "a bear of a test" and being "so cold that we nearly froze to death." Apparently the "lies" of literature are not only entertaining but useful in stating the truth.

I will discuss two levels at which the imagination tells the truth. Let me say at the outset that the arts do not always or necessarily or inherently or universally tell the truth. The imagination *did not escape the effects of the Fall*. But

---

*What I say in this paragraph has become a leading theme in recent literary theory. For typical treatments, see Roger Cardinal, *Figures of Reality: A Perspective on the Poetic Imagination* (London: Croom Helm, 1981); and T. E. Apter, *Fantasy Literature: An Approach to Reality* (Bloomington: Indiana University Press, 1982).

when the "lies" of the imagination tell the truth, they do so in the following ways.

To begin, let me return to the concreteness of the world of the imagination. By being so concrete, the arts tend overwhelmingly to tell us the truth about the physical world that we perceive around us. Even though poems are often not "about" the images that appear in the poems, there is a sense in which these poems do, however, put us into contact with these realities.

Knowledge of the Physical World

Whether knowledge of the physical world is worth having depends on one's values and world view. Plato, believing that the arts imitate only external reality as a mirror reflects objects, thought this type of knowledge was rather frivolous, a knowledge hardly worth having. True knowledge is abstract, said Plato, and we get it from mathematics and philosophy courses, not from art and literature courses.

A Christian viewpoint disagrees with this pagan denigration of physical reality. Things are real. They are real because God made them. And because He made them, they are important and worthy of study and even a proper type of love. Not only did God make things, He created us so that we perceive them as much through our physical senses as our minds. The color and smell of a rose are not irrelevant or illusory.

Jesus told people to "consider the lilies of the field" (Matt. 6:28). How do we do so? Certainly not without looking and smelling. The American painter Andrew Wyeth once told an interviewer, "I love to study the many things that grow below the corn stalks and bring them back into the studio to study the color. If one could only catch that true color of nature—the very thought of it drives me mad."[24] *That* is considering the lilies of the field.

So for all its far-flung fantasies, the imagination also paradoxically stays close to the way things are. Tolkien, in his classic essay entitled

"On Fairy-Stories," remarks that it was in the utterly fantastic world of the fairy tale that he first became fully aware of the physical world about him. He writes, "It was in fairy-stories that I first divined the potency of . . . things, such as stone, and wood, and iron; tree and grass; house and fire; bread and wine."[25]

Truthfulness to Human Experience and Reality

The second level at which the imagination tells the truth is the level of what I will call reality, or human experience, or issues. No matter how fantastic the details of an artistic work might be, the realities and issues and experiences that those details are intended to represent are real. Consider again the following diagram of how the arts work:

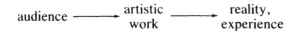

audience ⟶ artistic work ⟶ reality, experience

If we look only at the work, it contains much that is literally a lie: bigger-than-life statues, people and scenes made out of paint, talking trees, floating islands, people who speak in sonnet form, combinations of sounds that you will never hear if you go for a thousand walks in the woods. But we are not intended to look only *at* this imaginative construct. We also look *through* it to our experience in the world. The work of art is a veil or window or lens through which we look at reality. Let's turn to some illustrations.

Let me begin with one of the smallest of all literary units, the poetic *metaphor*. A metaphor compares one thing to another; in fact, it identifies one thing *with* another thing that it is literally not. A metaphor taken literally is always a lie. Consider, for example, the first verse of Psalm 1:

Blessed is the man
who walks not in the counsel of the wicked,
nor stands in the way of sinners,
nor sits in the seat of scoffers.

53

Imagination:
The "Lie" That
Tells the Truth

Look at the second line. The wicked do not literally take walks down a path called "the counsel of the wicked." They do not literally publish handbooks of wicked behavior or conduct legal seminars entitled "The Counsel of the Wicked." They do not even pass legislation called "the counsel of the wicked."

Again, according to the psalm, the godly person does not "stand in the way of sinners." On college campuses you will not find a field or room called "the way of sinners" where people stand together. And what about the picture of sitting "in the seat of scoffers"? People in a sarcastic mood do not literally go to the student center and take turns sitting in a chair with a sign over it that reads "the seat of scoffers."

Do these literal lies tell the truth? Yes they do. People do not literally take a walk down a wicked path, but the metaphor of the path or way implies the long-term nature of life, progress or change, and arrival at a destination, all of which are true of a person's life. There is not literally a journal called "the counsel of the wicked," but there are things called peer pressure and cultural influence that are as coercive as legislation. The image of sitting in the seat has political nuances in the Old Testament; it means to be a member of the policy-making body of a town. Wicked people are not the only ones who affect the law-making process, but they help to set an atmosphere that can have a detrimental influence on others.

Or consider the two *similes* that conclude the Sermon on the Mount (Matt. 7:24–27):

Every one then who hears these words of mine and does them will be like a wise man who built his house upon the rock; and the rain fell, and the floods came, and the winds blew and beat upon that house, but it did not fall, because it had been founded on the rock. And every one who hears these words of mine and does not do them will be like a foolish man who built his house upon the sand; and the rain fell, and the floods came, and the winds blew and beat against that house, and it fell; and great was the fall of it.

The passage is full of concrete objects (house, rock, sand, wind, rain, flood), but it is not *about* these things. Following Christ does not really mean building a house. But we can look *through* the picture *at* the reality of what it means to have a life based on what is solid and dependable.

If we turn from poetry and figures of speech to story, we find exactly the same principle at work. Flannery O'Connor, a Roman Catholic writer from rural Georgia, once said that "when you write fiction you are speaking *with* character and action, not *about* character and action."[26] If this is true, *about* what does a storyteller speak with character and action? The answer: life and reality. The particulars of the story are a fiction, but the realities they portray are true.

Consider, for example, that favorite ballad of high school and college English teachers, *The Rime of the Ancient Mariner*. Written by the English Romantic poet Samuel Taylor Coleridge, the poem is a haunting story of great imaginative power. In the poem the mariner takes a sea journey into a supernatural world where he does something very senseless. He shoots an albatross that had been hanging around the ship. The whole order of nature falls apart as a result of this crime, and in punishment the mariner is forced to wear the dead albatross around his neck.

The literal details of this story are preposterous. In real life people do not go around with a dead albatross around their necks. Not even on college campuses have you seen such a sight. But people do go to work or to the psychiatrist haunted by the horror of unrelieved guilt. The picture is so truthful, in fact, that our store of proverbs includes one that speaks of an albatross about our neck.

When the mariner in Coleridge's story blesses the water snakes that he is watching in the starlight, the albatross slides from his neck into the sea, and he is able to pray again. Nothing like this literally happens to people in the everyday world, but people do lose their guilt and experience the new life. So no matter how remote the world of Coleridge's poem may be from reality in its literal details, it is also so much a part of reality that every person carries that world within his or her own soul. Samuel Johnson, the great English writer and critic, was right, then, when he said that the details of literature "are not mistaken for realities but . . . bring realities to mind."[27]

The same thing is true of the other arts. When I was growing up in the 1950s, my baseball hero from that era was Stan Musial, the great hitter who played for the St. Louis Cardinals. Today there is a statue of "Stan the Man" outside Busch Stadium in St. Louis. It is elevated on a base seven or eight feet high, and the statue itself is several feet bigger than the person is in real life. At a literal level, the statue is another of the "lies" of art. Does this bigger-than-life representation tell the truth about its subject? Yes, it does. It captures the greatness of the athlete in a way that a book full of statistics about him does not.

The archetypes of literature are more simplified and more highly structured than what we find in the real world, but the patterns that they embody are realities in our own lives. We do, in fact, undergo initiations, undertake quests, and endure temptations. And as for the two lists of archetypes, one ideal and the other unideal, they are the most accurate picture we have of the longings and fears of the human race. They tell us more about some aspects of the human psyche than a psychology book does.

Summary: There Is More to Reality Than Facts

When people try to organize and express what they know to be true, they find that truth and reality cannot be adequately contained in abstract propositions and facts. That is why the human race has always turned to the imagination (literature and the arts) to express its beliefs and feelings. As Northrop Frye has written in one of the best books on the subject, "The constructs of the imagination tell us things about human life that we don't get in any other way."[28] Again, the "lies" of literature are a lens through which we look at reality. Like optical lenses or sunglasses or microscopes or telescopes or prisms, literature is a "distorting" mechanism that changes or rearranges factual reality so we can see it better.

The Importance of the Imagination for Christians

How does all this theory about the imagination relate to the interests of Christians? In the first place, Christians need to respect the primacy of imagination in art. They need to build their practice as producers and "consumers" of art on the best aesthetic theory that is available. Modern aesthetic theory is based on the imagination as the key to everything else.

The Christian community has not always respected the imaginative nature of the arts. The imagination works by incarnation, fleshing out images and ideas, and by indirection, letting the reader draw his or her own conclusions from the author's roundabout method of presentation (subtlety as opposed to didacticism). Do not Christian writers and film makers and artists in our day often have a debilitating tendency to be abstract rather than concrete, moralizing instead of moral, preachy rather than incarnational? Do they not have a fatal tendency to *spell it out*? And do not Christian consumers of the arts encourage such tendencies, indeed, even demand them?

And what about the imaginary element in the

arts? Do Christians in the arts feel more comfortable with biography than fiction or fantasy, or realism in painting rather than impressionism, or a newspaper rather than a novel? Francis Schaeffer has written that "Christian artists do not need to be threatened by fantasy and imagination. . . . The Christian is the one whose imagination should fly beyond the stars."[29]

God, the Imaginer

Christians, in fact, have a more convincing reason for relishing the imagination than the world at large may have. The Bible and the Christian faith based on it sanction the imagination as a valid form of knowing and expressing truth. God Himself is an imaginer. Look at the world He created: concrete, filled with creatures that we ourselves would never have thought up, plants that are fantastic rather than predictable. No computer would have produced the type of world that we encounter on a visit to the zoo. Christians who believe that God created the world need no apology for the imagination other than the character and work of God.

An interesting sidelight to the idea of God as the great imaginer occurs in connection with the type of robe that God commanded the priest to wear when he went into the Holy of Holies (Exod. 28:31–35). The robe included blue pomegranates. But in nature there are no blue pomegranates. The Christian is free to have imagination.

And what about the command in the Psalms to sing a *new* song to the Lord? Can we say that God is the great imaginer who is always busy creating something new and who expects His creatures to imagine new stories and metaphors and symphonies and statues? The idea of creation is a main pillar of Christian doctrine. If God created the universe out of nothing, Christians, of all people, should revel in human creativity—in the ability of people to create something that cannot be adequately explained by a previously existing model. Dorothy Sayers, in fact, wrote that the "idea of Art as *creation* is . . . the one important contribution that Christianity has made to aesthetics."[30]

The Example of the Bible

Next, looming large as a work of the imagination is the example of the Bible. Its most customary way of expressing God's truth is not the sermon or theological outline but the story, the poem, and the vision, all of them literary forms and products of the imagination. Think of how much biblical truth has been incarnated in character and event. Then pause to remember the poetry of the Bible, including the heavy incidence of symbol and metaphor even in the prose of the New Testament: "The LORD is my shepherd." "The mountains skipped like rams, the hills like lambs." "The tongue is a fire." "Put on the whole armor of God." And as for the visions of the prophets and the Book of Revelation, what could be more fantastic than some of those details?

When we turn from the Bible to the Christian world today, we cannot help but be struck by the contrast. The tendency today is to theologize everything. The theological abstraction and outline have replaced the imaginative boldness of the writers of the Bible. Our own culture, including the Christians in it, no longer trusts the power of metaphor or paint on canvas or music to express the truth. Jesus did not distrust the imagination. He told stories and spoke in metaphor and simile. We may safely conclude, therefore, that the Bible is a work of power, beauty, and imagination: a literary masterpiece. One thing which it definitely is *not* is a purely theological outline with proof texts attached.

We mislead ourselves if we ignore the importance of the imagination as an element in a person's world view. One of the commonest of all fallacies is that a person's world view consists only of ideas. One reason for the prevalence of this fallacy is that most of the people who write on the subject are philosophers with a bias toward abstract concepts.

**Imagination and
World View**

But a person's world view has a "mythology" as well as an ideology. It is comprised of images, symbols, stories, and characters, as well as ideas. People are as much *symbolic* creatures as *rational* ones. A noted theologian has said that

> we are far more image-making and image-using creatures than we usually think ourselves to be and . . . are guided and formed by images in our minds. . . . Man . . . is a being who grasps and shapes reality . . . with the aid of great images, metaphors, and analogies.[31]

Some of the commonest images in our world view are our storehouse of heroes—characters whose actions and values we admire and try to imitate. Such images of success—such models that we consider normative—exercise a powerful influence over how we live. Someone has analyzed the situation thus: "We make decisions mostly on the basis of images. . . . Our decisions are not made on facts; they are made on the way in which we see ourselves with the facts. This is 'imaging.' "[32] In a similar vein, another writer has suggested that we pattern our lives, not around a set of ideas, but a story:

> Each one of us has . . . an inner life story that we spend all our lives telling to ourselves alone. . . . Our inner life story is the content of our most private level of consciousness. It is the actual reason, the final basis of the decisions we make— decisions that are often so baffling to others.[33]

It is a commonplace that the stories that people and cultures tell and retell have the effect of guiding and reinforcing their values and actions.

All of this should be familiar to Christians, but I fear that it is not. The Bible is filled with images, stories, and characters as well as ideas. Christians live out their lives in an awareness of such doctrines as creation and sin and redemption, but also a host of specific images (cross, light, God as Shepherd) and stories. They organize their understanding and decisions around such images as Abraham and Ruth and the Good Samaritan and the father's forgiveness of the prodigal son. Jesus acknowledged the power of such images when He told His disciples to "remember Lot's wife" (Luke 17:32).

Example, as well as precept, governs our behavior. Do you remember the last time you tried to assemble an appliance or piece of equipment you had bought? If the directions included a good picture of what you were supposed to do, you may have not even used the instructions. The imagination serves a similar function in our lives.

Our imagination may govern our behavior more than ideas do. At the level of ideas, for example, we may know that true worth does not consist of physical possessions, but if our minds are filled with images of fancy cars and expensive clothes, our behavior will likely follow a materialistic path. We might *say* that God created the world, but if our minds are filled with images of random evolutionary processes, we will quickly start to think like evolutionists.

The imagination is a leading ingredient in our picture of truth. We live under its sway, whether we realize it or not. Literature (including such popular manifestations as movies or popular music) is one of the chief influences on our imagination. Literature provides much of the content of our imagination. It often tells the real truth about our inner selves and values more accurately than do the ideas that we assent to with our intellect.

Christians can also do themselves a favor by realizing the potential of the imagination to express religious truth. We may appropriate religious truth with our imagination as well as with our intellect.

The Imagination As a Means of Grace

Compare, for example, the experience of listening to a sermon with listening to Handel's *Messiah*. What is the difference? The sermon appeals mainly to our intellect, to our grasp of the facts. Handel's *Messiah,* whose words come from the Bible, also appeals to our grasp of the facts of salvation, but the music and the poetic arrangement of the words appeals to more than that. Listening to Handel's *Messiah* is a sensory and emotional experience that goes far beyond what happens if we only read the words or hear them spoken. We "take in" the truth about salvation with the combination of reason, emotion, and sensation that I call imagination.

Here is another comparison. We assimilate the statement in the Apostles' Creed that God is "Maker of heaven and earth" as a theological proposition. Compare your experience of that same truth when you go for a walk on a warm, sunny spring afternoon. The truth is the same in both cases, namely, that God is the Lord of creation, and that He made it good. But when you feel the sun, you know or experience that truth, not only with your intellect or as an abstraction, but with your senses, feelings, and imagination (that is, as an "image"). Truth does not come to us solely through our reason and intellect. It comes to us both ways in the Bible, which in some places is factual and abstract and theological in its approach to truth, and sometimes is imaginary and concrete in its approach.

A look at our church services says the same thing. They do not limit truth to the intellect. We experience religious truth through our senses when we hear and make music in a church service, or when we eat and drink in the sacrament of communion. We express and take in the truth visually when we decorate or place symbols in the sanctuary. The sermon appeals primarily to our minds. What we grasp with our minds is primary. The others build upon what we know through our reason. But we need and value all the ways in which we take in and "know" the truth.

SUMMARY

The imagination speaks a "language" all its own. It uses concrete images. It may make things up that are not factual or literal. It may heighten reality and organize it into one big story and divide it into contrasting halves.

For all its licenses, however, the imagination puts us in touch with the physical world around us and with common human experience. It also shows us what the human race wants and does not want and therefore tells us a lot about human nature and behavior.

A good drama can be as *true* as the evening news on television, even though it may be entirely fictional. A novel can be as *true* (to human experience in the world) as the daily newspaper. The news tells us what happened; the arts tell us what *happens*. Both are equally true, though in different ways.

Christians have every reason to value the potential of the imagination as a vehicle for knowing and expressing the truth, including religious truth. The imagination is one of the ways (though not the only way) by which people deal with truth, both in their daily lives and in their specifically religious experiences.

chapter three

Literature As Recreation

Literature is a form of recreation or entertainment. One of its goals is to give pleasure. The enjoyment of literature is a wise use of leisure time and one of the main functions of literature.

"Why don't you read something useful?" "Only lazy people read novels."

Such comments might come from an irritated roommate or a parent worried about a young person's reading habits. The argument is as old as Plato, who complained that literature is only "a kind of play or sport," not to be accepted unless it can be shown that "there is a use in poetry as well as a delight."[34]

Faced with the charge of the nonusefulness of literature, most defenders of literature have tried to meet the argument on its own terms and to

The Charge of Literature's Nonusefulness

63

show that literature is useful after all. It teaches truth. It moves people to good moral behavior. It helps a person build a world view.

There is plenty of truth in these arguments, as other chapters in this book suggest. But to defend literature only on these grounds is less impressive than we are sometimes led to think. It ignores *why* most people read a story or go to a play or movie. To defend literature for its usefulness also omits much that people who love literature value in it.

How We Know Literature Is a Form of Recreation

Along with the other things that we would wish to say in favor of literature, it needs to be said emphatically that literature is a form of recreation or entertainment. It possesses what someone has called "refreshment value." *It is the burden of this chapter to show that there is a sense in which literature has more in common with a ball game than a lecture, and is more like a stroll in a park than studying a textbook.* How do we know that literature is a form of entertainment?

1. The Experience of Readers

We can begin by observing *why* people take the time to read stories or poems or attend plays. The overwhelming majority of people (not counting those who are enrolled in a literature course or wish to impress a friend) go to literature for enjoyment and entertainment and refreshment. They read literature because they want to, not because they have to. The motivation for reading literature is different from that for reading an informational book.

We can also ask *when* people read literature or go to see a play. They do so during their leisure time: in the evening, on the weekend, during vacation. Even our posture and surroundings are typically relaxed when we read literature. We might normally read a textbook or an owner's manual at a desk or table, but we probably read a novel in an easy chair.

Another reason to classify literature as a form of recreation is to observe the effect that literature has on us when we read it. The works that we finish reading and later reread obviously strike us as pleasurable. The delight and appeal of stories, for example, is well known. One of the most universal human impulses can be summed up in the four words, "Tell me a story." It is no wonder that the English Renaissance poet and critic Sir Philip Sidney described the storyteller as someone with the enchanting power to hold "children from play, and old men from the chimney corner."[35] In a similar vein, Owen Barfield, British scholar and friend of C. S. Lewis, in speaking of the pleasures of poetry, describes "the old, authentic thrill, which is so strong that it binds some men to their libraries for a lifetime."[36] I remember how liberating I found a comment made by Charles Williams, the remarkably versatile English writer who was an inspiration to T. S. Eliot, C. S. Lewis, and Dorothy Sayers. Williams said that "*Paradise Lost* is much more fun written in blank verse than it would be in prose. . . . Let us have all the delights of which we are capable."[37]

2. The Testimony of Writers

But we don't have to take only the experience of readers as a basis for concluding that literature is intended to be fun. Writers say the same thing.

T. S. Eliot, the most important and influential poet of the twentieth century, called literature "superior amusement."[38] W. H. Auden, a contemporary British-born American poet, said that when young writers would tell him that they wanted to write poetry, he would ask, "Why do you want to write poetry?" According to Auden, "If the young man answers: 'I have important things I want to say,' then he is not a poet. If he answers: 'I like hanging around words listening to what they say,' then maybe he is going to be a poet."[39] Dylan Thomas, one of the greatest of modern poets, has said,

> I like to treat words as a craftsman does his wood or stone . . . , to hew, carve, mold, coil, polish, and plane them into patterns, sequences, sculptures, fugues of sound. . . . I, myself, do not read poetry for anything but pleasure.[40]

Writers do not, of course, claim that literature is *only* entertaining. Robert Frost expressed the majority viewpoint when he said that a work of literature "begins in delight and ends in wisdom. . . . It begins in delight . . . and ends in a clarification of life."[41] Notice the order in which the two functions occur. The reason why we go to literature in the first place is to enjoy ourselves. But afterwards we mull over the content of the work and analyze it and make intellectual sense of it. The useful and entertaining functions of literature are complementary, not incompatible.

3. The Nature of Literature Itself

Readers want literature to be an enjoyable use of leisure time. Writers claim to entertain us. But we could come to the same conclusion simply by looking at literature itself. Literature appeals to much besides our interest in ideas and content.

One way to test this claim is to substitute a summary of content for a story or poem or play. The summary does not satisfy us. We want the story or poem or play itself. We want something that only literary form and creativity and technique can give us. Even if we could gain the same truth from another piece of writing, we want the particular appeal and enjoyment of the literary work itself. C. S. Lewis has said in this connection that to regard a work of literature

> as primarily a vehicle for . . . philosophy is an outrage to the thing the poet has made for us. I use the words *thing* and *made* advisedly. . . . One of

the prime achievements in every good fiction has nothing to do with truth or philosophy or a *Weltanschauung* [world view] at all. . . . If entertainment means light and playful pleasure, then I think it is exactly what we ought to get from some literary work. . . . If it means those things which "grip" the reader of popular romance—suspense, excitement and so forth—then I would say that every book should be entertaining. A good book will be more; it must not be less.[42]

The Importance of Literary Form

The reason literature lends itself to enjoyment is not hard to find. Literature is an art form—a craft or skill. Robert Frost called poetry "a performance in words."[43] Literature is designed to please and awe us with its display of literary form and technique. Someone has said that "our primal aesthetical experience is . . . a response of enchantment to 'beauty' (in a very wide sense of the term)."[44] Another literary scholar, in surveying the three areas where modern criticism has attempted to find the value of literature, describes one of the areas as "a group of closely related ideas about form, which is . . . treated as a . . . function of the imagination: beauty, form, art, style, craftsmanship, structure, the perfect and isolated object."[45]

Literary "form" should be defined as anything that falls under the heading of *how* a piece of literature is put together, as distinct from *what* it says. Such form is an essential part of literature. Writers flaunt their skill with words and story structure and verse forms. Writing is a skill that we should admire, just as we admire the skill of an athlete or musician or artist. The craftsmanship that we can find in a story or poem always claims a big share of the attention that we give to it, for the simple reason that such technique is a major ingredient of literature.

Artistic joy or delight is one of the purposes of literature. The purpose of expository writing such as a newspaper article or textbook is purely practical. Such writing exists to point beyond itself to a body of information. Literature, by contrast, always adds an aesthetic purpose to the practical one. Its very form aims to give pleasure. Literary style calls attention to itself in a way that expository writing does not.

Writers know this very well. Ernest Hemingway rewrote the conclusion to *A Farewell to Arms* seventeen times in an effort to "get it right." Dylan Thomas made over two hundred manuscript versions of his poem "Fern Hill." The nineteenth-century Christian poet Gerard Manley Hopkins claimed that the form of a poem exists "for its own sake and interest even over and above its interest of meaning."[46] It is quite obvious that ordinary forms of discourse are not as preoccupied with craftsmanship and beauty as is literature. C. S. Lewis has said of literature that "every episode, explanation, description, dialogue—ideally every sentence—must be pleasurable for its own sake."[47]

There is no need to be scared off by the idea of literary form or artistry. It consists of the things that keep coming up in literature courses and that send teachers of literature into such ecstasy. Some of the underlying principles of artistic beauty (equally evident in music and painting, incidentally) are unity, centrality or focus, progression, repetition or recurrence, variation, contrast, balance, and rhythm. Another important aspect of literary form is literary genre ("kind," "type"), each with its own craft. The three major genres are story, drama, and poetry. But the term *form* also covers such diverse elements of literature as the sonnet form or epic style or satire or tragedy.*

It is not my aim to describe or illustrate the

---

*The nature and value of literary form have received superb recent treatment by Austin M. Wright, *The Formal Principle in the Novel* (Ithaca: Cornell University Press, 1982). This book is a helpful corrective to some modern critical trends that denigrate the element of form and beauty in literature.

myriad of techniques by which literature becomes entertaining and pleasurable. Any good literature course has this as a main purpose.* My concern is to offer some reasons why it is entirely proper for us to indulge our literary tastes for the sake of entertainment, pleasure, and beauty.

Literature As a Leisure Activity

Any complete discussion of the topic must sooner or later touch upon the bigger issue of leisure. Literature and the arts are something we cultivate after the basic needs of existence have been met. What can we say about the value of literature as a leisure pursuit?

Approached on purely human grounds, there can be little question that people need leisure for physical and emotional well-being. People who never take time off have physical and emotional breakdowns.†

Every well-balanced person devotes time to leisure pursuits. The question then becomes, What constitutes a *worthwhile* use of leisure time? There is no one right answer. But in view of the qualities of literature that I noted in earlier chapters, literature has much to commend it as a leisure activity. In a day of mindless leisure pursuits, literature stands out by engaging our mind. It awakens our imagination and frees us

*There is also a whole category of "introduction to literature" books. The best of these are probably those by Laurence Perrine, all published by Harcourt Brace Jovanovich: *Sound and Sense* (poetry), *Story and Structure* (narrative fiction), and *Literature: Structure, Sound, and Sense* (poetry, narrative, and drama in a single volume).

†The importance of literature in the average person's life is a lot easier to establish if we dignify leisure and recreation with the significance and honor they deserve. Some good general treatments include these: J. Huizenga, *Homo Ludens: A Study of the Play-Element in Culture* (1950; reprint, Boston: Beacon Press, 1955); Max Kaplan, *Leisure in America* (New York: John Wiley and Sons, 1960); Sebastian de Grazia, *Of Time, Work, and Leisure* (Leiden: E. J. Brill, 1974); James S. Hans, *The Play of the World* (Amherst: University of Massachusetts Press, 1981).

from our own time and place. It enriches our life by making us aware of the world within and without. It makes us sensitive to human experience and human fears and longings (in other words, basic human nature). The key to the enlightened use of leisure is education, broadly defined. We do in our leisure time what we have learned to do. We can upgrade the quality of our leisure time by learning to value what is excellent rather than mediocre. If left to ourselves, the law of mental laziness takes over and our horizons remain rather narrow.

Aristotle claimed that the goal of education was the wise use of leisure time. This is surely an overstatement, but one of the best tests of whether a person is truly educated is what he or she does with leisure time. Pascal, the seventeenth-century French philosopher, made a comment that I have seen verified again and again: "All the unhappiness of men arises from one single fact, that they cannot stay quietly in their own chamber."[48]

According to John Milton, the Puritan poet, a "complete and generous education" is one that equips a person to perform "all the offices, both private and public," that life affords.[49] In our economically oriented society, we are preoccupied with our public roles, chiefly the one of work (i.e., our job or profession). But what about the private role of living an enriching life of the mind and imagination? Reading good literature offers some appealing possibilities here.

An education is adequate only if it equips a person to spend an evening doing something more than listening to the kind of music or watching the type of television program that most people in our society are satisfied with. If you are a college student, I hope that you will pay particular attention to what I am saying. Compared with your college years, no other phase of life is likely to provide the same luxury of opportunity to broaden your horizons and develop your capacity for meaningful kinds of recreation. A literature course can have lifelong benefits if you will let it.

The Necessity of Beauty

If leisure can be defended on generally human grounds, so can artistic beauty. We live in a very utilitarian world that prizes what is useful and that in many ways despises what is not. But the human urge for beauty lives on. Look at the room around you. The colors that you see, and the pictures on the wall, do not serve a necessary function. Nevertheless, someone went to the trouble to supply them. By purely utilitarian standards, we could all wear only gray clothes, or produce only brown cars. But our artistic tastes won't let us do so.

To understand such a state of affairs, we need only appeal to human nature. This is exactly what Matthew Arnold did. "When we set ourselves to enumerate the powers which go to the building up of human life," he wrote, we find that "they are the power of conduct, the power of intellect and knowledge, the power of beauty, and the power of social life and manners." The important point that Arnold made is this:

> human nature is built up by these powers; we have the need for them all. . . . We feel the impulse for relating our knowledge to our sense for conduct and to our sense for beauty. . . . Such is human nature.[50]

Many of the most worthwhile things in life are of no practical use. Human nature nevertheless values them because they are beautiful. People continue to flock from the world of asphalt parking lots to the world of parks and gardens. Even many of those who greatly prefer urban life on a daily basis, periodically find themselves turning from concrete and skyscrapers to beaches and mountains with a great sense of relief and satisfaction.

Are facts more important than beauty? Computer mania may mislead us. We live in a world increasingly full of facts and statistics, but a lot of them are much less useful than we are led to believe. Behind the modern disparagement of the arts is the premise that facts are important because they are useful, while human creativity and beauty are useless. But not all facts are as useful as is claimed in our utilitarian age, and I would appeal to human nature to support my claim that people have important needs besides factual knowledge. The experience of beauty is one of them.

A Christian View of Beauty and Pleasure

Thus far I have defended artistic enjoyment and beauty on generally human grounds. Does Christianity have anything distinctive to say on the same subjects? It does—more than for any other chapter in this book. A person with a Christian world view values beauty and the enlightened use of leisure time in a way that contemporary society at large does not. Christians, therefore, are the last people in the world who should feel guilty about legitimate enjoyment or a zest for life.

1. The Doctrine of Creation

Several Christian doctrines form the basis for this endorsement of enjoyment and beauty. Perhaps the most important is the doctrine of creation. Christians believe that God is "Maker of heaven and earth." The Bible tells us, moreover, that people were created in the image (likeness) of God (Gen. 1:27).

How are people like God? There are several answers, but in the context where the statement appears in the Bible, the idea of creativity leaps out at once. "Had the author of Genesis anything particular in his mind when he wrote?" asks Dorothy Sayers in her famous book *The Mind of the Maker*. Her conclusion: "The characteristic common to God and man is apparently . . . the desire and the ability to make things."[51]

Can you or a friend justify the time involved in taking a course in fiction writing or poetry writing? Is your conscience clear when you spend several hours reading a novel? A Christian thinker has written, "As image-bearer of God, man possesses the possibility both to create something beautiful and to delight in it."[52] A Christian poet has commented that writers and artists can see themselves "as a kind of earthly assistant to God . . . , carrying on the delegated work of creation, making the fullness of creation fuller."[53]

We might also note the precise kind of world that God created. We need only look around us to see that He made a world that is beautiful as well as functional. From a utilitarian point of view, God did not have to create a world filled with colors and beautiful shapes. He could have created everything in a drab gray color, or He could have created people color-blind. It is obvious that God made provision for the quality of human life, not simply its survival. We read in Genesis 2:9 that when God created Paradise, the perfect environment for people, He "made to grow every tree that is pleasant to the sight and good for food." A double concern, you will note—both functional and aesthetically beautiful. The conditions for human well-being have not changed from that moment in Paradise.

2. The Example of the Bible

We can come to the same conclusion if we will look at the example of the Bible (in addition to its doctrine). God could have revealed Himself to people in a book devoid of literary beauty. Instead, we have the Bible, a book that a famous antagonist of Christianity called "unquestionably the most beautiful book in the world."[54]

If the message were all that mattered in the Bible, we might well wonder whether the biblical poets did not have something better to do with their time than put their utterances into the form of poetic parallelism and apt metaphors. The very example of the Bible leads us to conclude that in God's economy these poets did *not* have something better to do with their time and ability than to be artistic to the glory of God. The writer of Ecclesiastes speaks for the other biblical authors as well as for himself when he tells us that he arranged his material "with great care," and that he "sought to find pleasing words [words of delight]" (Eccles. 12:9–10).

3. The Biblical Attitude Toward Beauty

We also learn a lot when we read about Old Testament places of worship. Here we find emphatically that God values beauty. He put it into "the heart of the king, to beautify the house of the LORD" (Ezra 7:27). Even more explicit are the passages in Exodus 35–39 that describe the building of the Tabernacle. We read here that it was God Himself who called the chief artist and "filled him with the Spirit of God, with ability, with intelligence, with knowledge, and with all craftsmanship, to devise artistic designs, to work in gold and silver and bronze, in cutting stones for setting, and in carving wood, for work in every skilled craft" (Exod. 35:31–33). The same claim is extended to the other artists who beautified the Tabernacle (Exod. 35:35; see also Exod. 39:4).

The Bible encourages us to believe that beauty is divine in its origin and one of God's perfections. We read in the New Testament that "every good endowment and every perfect gift is from above, coming down from the Father of lights" (James 1:17). When we find beauty in literature (and in nature), we need not doubt where it comes from: it comes ultimately from God. Everything that we know about the character of God should purge from our minds at once that He is the author of ugliness rather than beauty, or that He values ugliness rather than beauty.

The Bible endorses pleasure and enjoyment as thoroughly as it approves of beauty. Pleasure and its synonyms are, for example, one of the recurrent themes in the Psalms. The writer of Psalm 16 rejoices in the fact that "the lines have fallen for me in pleasant places" (v. 6) and asserts that at God's "right hand are pleasures for evermore" (v. 11). For another poet the "harp with the psaltery" is "pleasant" (Ps. 81:2 KJV). And another psalm declares about God's people, "They feast on the abundance of thy house, and thou givest them drink from the river of thy delights" (Ps. 36:8). God is not opposed to pleasure.

One of the unifying themes of the Book of Ecclesiastes is the contrast between the false, purely humanistic pursuit of pleasure and the legitimate, God-oriented quest for pleasure. Two of the key assertions about the legitimacy of pleasure when it is placed in a context of faith in God are these:

> I know that there is nothing better for them than to be happy and enjoy themselves as long as they live; also that it is God's gift to man that every one should eat and drink and take pleasure in all his toil (Eccl. 3:12–13).

> Behold, what I have seen to be good and to be fitting is to eat and drink and find enjoyment in all the toil with which one toils under the sun the few days of his life which God has given him, for this is his lot. Every man also to whom God has given wealth and possessions and power to enjoy them, and to accept his lot and find enjoyment in his toil— this is the gift of God (Eccl. 5:18–19).

These same sentiments are reiterated in a classic New Testament passage in which Paul comments on wealthy people. Paul's advice to Timothy is as follows: "Charge them that are rich in this world, that they be not highminded, nor trust in uncertain riches, but in the living God, who giveth us richly all things to enjoy"

(1 Tim. 6:17 KJV). This key verse establishes three important principles: (1) God is the giver of all good things, (2) He gives people these things to enjoy, and (3) the misuse of them consists not in enjoyment of them but in trusting them or making idols of them.

The biblical doctrine of heaven also exalts pleasure. If heaven is the place where there is no more pain (Rev. 21:4), C. S. Lewis can correctly assert that "all pleasure is in itself a good and pain in itself an evil; if not, then the whole Christian tradition about heaven and hell and the passion of our Lord seems to have no meaning."[55]

No one could have lived a busier life than Jesus did during the years of His public ministry. Yet He did not reduce life to continuous work or evangelism. We never get the feeling that He was in a hurry, and we read frequently of His withdrawing into the wilderness. He must have enjoyed nature immensely. Yet He had a busy social life as well. If we could arrange the Gospel accounts of Jesus' habitual activities into a series of portraits, one of them would be a picture of Jesus attending a dinner or party. We read about Jesus eating dinner with Matthew (Matt. 9:10), a Pharisee (Luke 7:36), "a ruler who belonged to the Pharisees" (Luke 14:1), Zacchaeus (Luke 19:1–10), and Mary, Martha, and Lazarus (John 12:1–2). He turned water into wine to keep a wedding party going (John 2:1–10). By His example, Jesus consecrated pleasure and enjoyment, and gave a basis for our agreeing with John Calvin that "if we ponder to what end God created food, we shall find that he meant not only to provide for necessity but also for delight and good cheer."[56]

A person's attitude toward pleasure is actually a comment on his or her estimate of God. To assume that God dislikes pleasure and enjoyment is to charge Him with being sadistic toward His creatures. The Bible, of course, does not allow such a conclusion. As Norman Geisler, professor of systematic theology at Dallas Theological Seminary, writes, "God is not a celestial Scrooge who hates to see his children enjoy themselves. Rather, he is the kind of Father who is ready to say, 'Let us eat and make merry; for this my son was dead and is alive again; he was lost and is found' " (Luke 15:24).[57]

All that I have said about the Bible's approval of beauty and pleasure needs, of course, to be qualified. It would be easy to adduce dozens of biblical passages that make it clear that beauty and pleasure can be used in evil and destructive ways. These qualities are created and given by God and are good in principle. Like any of God's gifts, they can be perverted to a bad end by fallen people. That is why nineteenth-century Russian novelist Fyodor Dostoyevsky has one of his literary characters say that beauty is the battlefield where God and the devil fight for the human heart. Similarly, English novelist Aldous Huxley once wrote, "As a matter of plain historical fact, the beauties of holiness have often been matched and indeed surpassed by the beauties of unholiness."[58] What we are talking about, though, is the abuse of something, not its inherent nature.

The Christian's Invitation to Enjoy Literature

What does the biblical affirmation of beauty and pleasure have to do with the reading of literature? Primarily it validates the enjoyment of the imaginative beauty of literature as a Christian activity. Scripture tells us that people are created in the image of God. This means, among other things, that they have the ability to make something beautiful and to delight in it. *This is the biblical aesthetic; thus, when we enjoy the beauty of a sonnet or the magnificent artistry of an epic or the fictional inventiveness of a novel, we are enjoying a quality of which God is the ultimate source and performing an act similar to God's enjoyment of the beauty of His own creation.* To the question, "How do we read literature to the glory of God?" one good answer is, "By enthusiastically enjoying the artistic beauty of the literature that we read, recognizing God as the ultimate source of the beauty that we enjoy."

The way to show gratitude for a gift is to enjoy it. Any parent knows that the only real gratitude he or she desires from a child who has received a gift is simply the enthusiastic enjoyment of the gift. If artistic beauty and delight are, as the Bible implies, a gift of God, we can scarcely demonstrate our gratitude for the gift any more adequately than by using and enjoying it.

If the act of enjoying something beautiful seems either blameworthy or trivial, it is because we have fallen prey to an unbiblical attitude, whether it be derived from Platonism or asceticism or a perverted work ethic or scientific utilitarianism. The biblical attitude is well summarized in the statement of a missionary to India who wrestled with the question of the place of beauty in her missionary work. Her final conclusion:

> I believe my attitude toward beauty and order, as reflected in my home and lifestyle, says much to the people around me about the God I serve. Therefore, I want to reflect . . . something of the artistry, the beauty, the order of the one I'm representing, and in whose image I've been made. To me, sacrifice does not mean ugliness.[59]

Distinguishing Between Literary Form and Content

To believe in the legitimacy of enjoying artistic form and beauty is liberating. It allows Christian readers of literature to affirm the value of literature whose content or world view they may dislike or abhor. If God is the source of all beauty and artistry, then the artistic dimension of literature is the point at which Christian readers can be unreserved in their enthusiasm for the works of non-Christian writers. John Milton gradually came to deplore the ethical viewpoint of pagan authors, but he notes that "their art I still applauded."[60]

Failure to distinguish between the levels of form and content has led to two significant errors. On the one hand, it has led Christian readers who want to avoid being provincial in their tastes to endorse, at the level of ideas or viewpoint, works that no reader of discernment should claim to be consonant with Christianity. And on the other hand, Christian readers who have shown good judgment in measuring non-Christian attitudes in literature by a Christian standard have unfortunately devalued or rejected works that can offer much to a Christian's literary experience. The corrective to both errors is to distinguish the artistic from the moral/intellectual response and to be unreserved in affirming the value of non-Christian literature at the level of craftsmanship and beauty. Christians are rightly offended when non-Christians show no respect for the artistic skill of a Christian artist simply because of their antagonism to the artist's Christianity. It is just as deplorable when Christian readers do not respect and appreciate the *literary* excellence of non-Christian literature.

The Christian doctrine of stewardship also deserves comment. It means that we are responsible for the wise use of all that God has given us, including our leisure time.* C. S. Lewis has written this about the moral significance of choosing good leisure pursuits:

Christian Stewardship in Leisure Pursuits

> Our leisure, even our play, is a matter of serious concern. There is no neutral ground in the universe; every square inch, every split second, is claimed by

---

*Some excellent treatments of leisure from a Christian perspective include these: Robert Lee, *Religion and Leisure in America* (Nashville: Abingdon Press, 1964); Harold D. Lehman, *In Praise of Leisure* (Scottdale, Pa.: Herald Press, 1974); Josef Pieper, *Leisure: The Basis of Culture* (New York: New American Library, 1952, 1963).

God and counterclaimed by Satan. . . . It is a serious matter to choose wholesome recreations.[61]

Leisure, in other words, is an arena of choice in which we exercise good or bad stewardship. Frank Gaebelein, noted Christian author and educator, has said that "the very word 'leisure' implies responsibility. . . . Leisure and working time are equally to be accounted for to the Lord."[62]

In his book *The Restoration of Meaning to Contemporary Life*, Paul Elmen analyzed the modern cultural malaise that is particularly evident in the leisure pursuits of many people.[63] Some of the manifestations of the malaise are: boredom, the search for distraction, the fear of spending time alone, sensuality, escape into comedy, violence, and the appeal of horror ("the fun of being frightened"). Given the contemporary crisis in finding wholesome leisure pursuits, the reading of good quality literature is one of the Christian's best allies.

SUMMARY

Our practical modern world has regarded beauty and human creativity as an extraneous luxury. But if we look honestly and deeply within the human spirit as created by God, we will find a hunger for beauty. And if we look beyond the human spirit to the God of the Bible and the God of creation, we will conclude that God does not regard beauty as the unnecessary pursuit of an idle moment.

Literature is one of the things that can satisfy our urge for the enjoyment of beauty. Writers place a high value on technique and craftsmanship. They aim to please as well as edify, and they construct their works accordingly. As a result, literature is a form of recreation and a type of entertainment.

To spend leisure time in enriching ways is something that God expects of Christians. A Christian playwright was once asked why he wrote plays and responded, "For the glory of God and for fun." C. S. Lewis has written that the Christian "has no objection to comedies that merely amuse and tales that merely refresh. . . . We can play, as we can eat, to the glory of God."[64]

chapter four

How Writers Influence Their Audience

Writers aim to communicate to an audience. They are people with a vision of how things are or should be. They convey that vision through the literary work. Works of literature have a persuasive strategy embodied within them. Writers compose their works in such a way as to influence an audience to share their viewpoint.

Before looking at the role of the writer in the literary experience, we should stop to get the big picture. Whenever we attend a play or sit down to read a story or poem, there are four ingredients at work. They can be diagrammed as shown on the following page.[65]

At the center of it all is the work itself (the words on the page). It is the creation of a writer. A writer, in turn, gets material from the existing

The Four Elements of Literature

83

world, including the words, images, settings, characters, events, and experiences that make up the content of the work. And finally, the audience or reader is the one who assimilates the work.

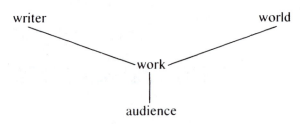

Various "approaches" to literature can be plotted on this diagram, and this will help to explain what goes on in a given literature course or critical essay. *Formalist criticism* focuses on the work itself and bases its commentary on the text rather than outside material. Critics who look upon literature as an *"imitation" of life* stress the relationships between a work and real life, including the specific ideas that were common in the writer's society and age. *Biographical criticism* emphasizes the connections between the writer and the work, including the intention of the writer. The most recent trend in literary criticism is *reader-centered criticism*, which focuses on the effect of literature on the audience and the role of the reader in the literary enterprise.

There is no single "correct" approach to literature. All four elements in the diagram, and their connections, are part of a complete study of literature. The purpose of the present chapter is to explore the importance of the writer in our experience of literature. All of our literary experiences involve an interaction between writer and audience, who together "create" the story or poem or play. This chapter and the next one, which deals with the role of the reader, are two halves of a single thing. (You should not, therefore, expect me to say in this chapter what belongs in the next chapter.)

What do writers do? We can divide their work into three components. (1) Writers *create* an artistic object (story, poem, play) that possesses elements of artistic form. (2) Writers *present* an aspect of human experience for the reader's contemplation. (3) Writers *interpret* the experiences that they present.

The Writer's Task

A writer's philosophic or moral outlook is less influential with the first two activities than with the third. The ability to write in poetic form or to construct a good story is a skill that is the same for all writers, regardless of their philosophic bias. Although a writer's world view affects what he or she selects for portrayal, the subject of literature for any writer is potentially all of life, and the ability to use words to paint the exact contours of a given human experience requires the same skill with words for any writer. But the interpretation that writers give to the human experiences they portray depends from start to finish on their world view, and it is this aspect of the writer's task that I will discuss in this chapter.

This chapter might well be subtitled "Literature as Communication." It is based on the premise that writers view their works as a way of communicating with an audience. They have something that they wish to say to others. They do not ordinarily write a story or poem and then throw it into the wastebasket. They hope to have readers, and the more the better.

Literature as Communication

The point at which the writer and reader meet

is, of course, the work itself. We can picture the process of literary communication like this:

writer ⎯⎯⎯⎯⎯→ work ⎯⎯⎯⎯⎯→ audience

The Importance of a Writer's Perspective

Like anyone else, writers view the world from their own perspective and from their own range of experiences. They select the material for their literary works on the basis of what they know about life, and they mold their material according to their beliefs. Joyce Cary, a contemporary British novelist, has summarized the matter well:

> All great artists have a theme, an idea of life profoundly felt and founded in some personal and compelling experience. . . . A novelist, therefore, can give only . . . truth with an angle. . . . The writer selects his facts. He arranges their order to suit his own conception of values, his own theme.[66]

The writer's "slant" on life is usually called the *theme* of a work.

Sometimes a writer's theme is very specific. An antiwar poem, for example, is usually a protest against a particular historical situation and reflects a particular philosophic position on war. A novel like *The Grapes of Wrath*, John Steinbeck's Depression era classic, deals with specific types of oppression and injustice at a particular time in American history. A nature poem by the English Romantic poet William Wordsworth is more universal, but here, too, the writer has a clear theme (the beauty and healing effect of nature).

Often, however, a writer aims to communicate what I will call a general sense of life. Such literature may simply affirm or celebrate certain human values, such as love, home, or friendship. Or it may wish to assert in general terms that "this is the way life is." In such cases, there is no need to force a work into specific thematic statements.

Regardless of whether a writer's theme is general or specific, it is an inevitable part of literature. Storytellers, for example, do more than entertain an audience; someone has rightly said that to tell a story "is to create a world, adopt an attitude, suggest a behavior."[67] Similarly, lyric poets put their feelings and reflections into words and then publish their poems because they think that their feelings and reflections are worth sharing with others.

The fact that writers have something to say results in a persuasive element in literature. The writer's attempt to influence a reader is not equally strong in every work, but at the very least writers have conscious designs on their readers. Their aim is *affective:* they try to affect their readers in calculated ways. Modern British literary critic David Lodge has said that "the writer expresses what he knows by affecting the reader; the reader knows what is expressed by being receptive to effects."[68] Writers aim to make the audience share their vision—to see what they see, feel what they feel, and interpret life as they do. They arrange their works in such a way as to make us approve of some things and disapprove of others. They constantly try to make readers or viewers commit themselves as they proceed through a work.

How do writers achieve this persuasive aim? Recall the diagram of how writers communicate to an audience:

writer ⟶ work ⟶ audience

Obviously, whatever gets communicated must be embodied in the work itself. Recall, too, that literature has its own forms or "language."

Storytellers speak *through* characters, events, and settings. Poets communicate *through* images, metaphors, and other figures of speech. The purpose of the next several pages is to explore some of the ways in which writers use literary techniques to influence an audience.

Although some reader-centered criticism has tried to banish the writer from the literary scene, I would suggest that we can profitably view the writer as our traveling companion through a work. Writers arrange what we will see. They point out things along the way. Sometimes they speak to us directly about what we are looking at, telling us how to interpret what is before us. As readers we are not obliged to see *only* what our tour guide points to, but it would be foolish to ignore the writer's presence in the work.

How Writers Influence You

What are the *persuasive devices* (also called "rhetorical devices" or "rhetorical strategies") by which writers influence an audience?

1. Controlling What You See and Don't See

We can begin at the most fundamental level of all, that of *subject matter.* Simply by what writers choose to write about (and therefore cause the reader to observe and think about), they are already making a comment on reality and human values. By the very act of reading something, we have committed ourselves to the value of thinking about and experiencing the specific aspect of life that the writer has set before us. We have also agreed to place ourselves temporarily under the partial control of the author.

What writers omit can be as important as what they include. Writers who continually make us look at the sordid side of life are by that very selection of material conveying a sense of life. The English poet William Wordsworth once wrote a springtime nature poem in which he catalogued only the beautiful sights and sounds that he experienced on a walk in the woods. We

have no difficulty in identifying his outlook as "romantic." A century later, the English novelist and poet Thomas Hardy parodied Wordsworth's poem by describing a similar walk in the woods. Hardy omitted all that is positive in nature and instead described plants and animals struggling against each other for survival. Such selectivity is obviously a "naturalistic" viewpoint.

Both poems are examples of what psychologists call *selective perception*. Every work of literature is the product of selective perception, and as readers we need to be aware of this.

2. The Effect of Alternatives Within a Work

As readers or viewers, we are forced to pay attention to what a writer puts before us. Once we have committed ourselves to read a given work or watch a play, we are a captive audience. Because of this, readers are strongly influenced by the *presence or absence of the alternatives* that writers can put into their stories and poems if they choose to do so.

For example, consider *Utopia* by Thomas More, the English Lord Chancellor beheaded by Henry VIII. In this work the fictional main character is Hythloday, a traveler who extols the merits of an ideal state he had visited in his travels. At the end of the book, the narrator of the whole work steps forward and tells us that he partly disagrees with Hythloday's enthusiasm for the Utopian way of life. Given this encouragement by the work itself, the reader finds it much easier to criticize Utopia than if Hythloday were given the last word. A story that includes a foil (contrast) to a given viewpoint produces a different effect from one that omits such an alternative.

3. Choosing Sides

Aside from considerations of what a writer includes and excludes from a work, the most common way by which writers influence a reader is *to construct situations in which a reader has to exercise approval or disapproval, sympathy or aversion.* This is most easily seen in stories, where we are always forced to take sides for or against characters in the story, or to approve or disapprove of what a character says or does.

Reading a poem is very similar. Is this scene positive or negative? Do I like or dislike this sentiment? How do I feel about the viewpoint that is being offered for my approval? Such questions of sympathy and aversion keep coming up as we read even short poems.

4. Evaluative Descriptions

Another way in which writers control how we respond to the content of what they put before us is by the *evaluative terminology* they use when describing scenes, characters, or events. When Milton, in the middle of his sonnet on his blindness, refers to the meditation that he has just dramatized as "that murmur," we know that he intends us to view his earlier despair and rebellion against God's providence as something negative. It is "that" murmur, not "my" murmur (implying distance from it), and by calling it a "murmur" Milton alludes to the wicked complaints of the Israelites against what God had sent in the biblical Book of Exodus. George Herbert, the seventeenth-century English poet and pastor, wrote a poem ("The Collar") that expresses rebellion against God for thirty-two lines, only to evaluate that rebellion negatively in the last four lines, which begin with the words, "But as I raved and grew more fierce and wild / At every word. . . ."

5. Repetition

One of the most effective ways in which writers control a reader's response is by the technique of *repetition.* By repeatedly calling our attention to a given phenomenon, a writer controls how we assimilate the material. For example, notice how often the Irish novelist James Joyce draws our attention to the hopelessness of life in Dublin in the opening paragraph of his short story "Araby," a story about a young boy's frustrated first infatuation:

> North Richmond Street, being blind [a dead end street], was a quiet street except at the hour when the Christian Brothers' School set the boys free. An uninhabited house of two storeys stood at the blind end, detached from its neighbors in a square ground. The other houses of the street, conscious of decent lives within them, gazed at one another with brown imperturbable faces.

By repeating such motifs as blindness, bondage, and detachment, the author has already set an atmosphere and told us what will be important in the view of life portrayed in the story.

6. Highlighting

A literary audience is also heavily influenced to share the writer's viewpoint when the writer *highlights* certain features in a work. Most literature gives us a heightened version of a given subject. *Exaggeration* is one means of such highlighting. In literature, people in love are ideally beautiful, heroes are ideally heroic, villains are worse than people usually are, and so forth. These are conventions of literature, a literary "code language" that serves the purpose of getting us to notice exactly what the writer wishes us to see about life.

Another way of highlighting something is to *omit things,* leaving only the central feature for us to see. A naturalist like Thomas Hardy, for example, distills the misery of life and tries to convince us that life is exactly as bad as he claims by portraying only the negative side of life.

7. Foregrounding

The concept of *"foregrounding"* also explains how writers get us to see things from their perspective. In works of literature, things of lesser importance recede into the background, while others force themselves on a reader's attention. This process is usually called "foregrounding." In Jesus' parable of the Good Samaritan, for example, the traveler who is robbed remains anonymous and vaguely drawn; he is simply "a certain man" because the point of the parable does not rest on him. The Samaritan, however, is not only identified by nationality, but in the original Greek, forty-six words are devoted to what happens before the Samaritan arrives on the scene and sixty to his behavior after he arrives. All of the other characters in the story become the "background" against which the really important figure and action are "foregrounded."

8. Context and Contrast

The *context* into which a detail is put also influences us. In a movie, the presence of harmonious or discordant background music influences how we respond to a scene. *Contrast* or *foil* (something that "sets off" a detail) is one of the commonest ways of providing a context in literature. Just as in real life a short person's lack of height becomes pronounced when he or she is put beside a tall person, writers regularly use foils to direct our perspective. In Shakespeare's *Macbeth*, for example, we see the full horror of Macbeth's evil partly because the writer sets it over against the integrity of various good characters. The despair that is voiced in Hardy's poem "The Darkling Thrush" is made all the sharper by being contrasted to the joyful song of a bird.

9. The Importance of the Ending

Writers not only select the details that we view; they also *arrange* those details in a carefully calculated way. The way in which a story or poem *ends* is especially crucial in determining its overall meaning. In a story, one or more characters undertake an experiment in living. The mere fact that the story portrays a given experience does not imply that the author approves of it. In the overwhelming majority of instances, the way in which stories end is the key to interpreting how writers view the characters and actions that they themselves have arranged. Even short poems are capable of reversing things at the end.

This "rule of end stress" means that as readers we must view works of literature as a *whole* before we interpret their final meaning. It is true that writers set up signposts along the way, but in many cases we need to revise our understanding as the work unfolds. The conclusion of most works of literature casts a retrospective light over what has preceded.

Poetic justice, in which good characters are rewarded and bad ones punished, is a nearly universal impulse among storytellers. This narrative convention is open to criticism, because in real life such justice is often lacking. But it may be that writers are attracted to poetic justice, not because they think that life is always just, but because it is an indirect, literary way of showing what behavior they think is good and bad. They end their stories with reward and punishment as a way of influencing how a reader interprets the work as a whole.

10. Moments of Epiphany

Storytellers also tend to structure stories around one or more moments of *epiphany* ("revelation," "insight"). Usually there is an epiphany near the end of the story. As the very word suggests, an epiphany is usually a tip-off to the main meaning of a story—a comment about what it all adds up to. At the end of Joyce's story "Araby," the adolescent hero whose first infatuation has just ended in defeat gazes up into the darkness and sees himself "as a creature driven and derided by vanity." From start to finish, the story has given us variations on exactly this theme of the world as hostile and victimizing. In the short story "Odor of Chrysanthemums" by twentieth-century English author D. H. Lawrence, we know exactly what the story means when the wife of the deceased miner, looking at the corpse of her husband, is aware for the first time that she had always been so conscious of his failings as a husband that she never saw him as a person.

11. Direct Statement

The persuasive devices that I have noted thus far are mainly indirect ways by which a writer influences an audience. But authors also exercise the option of entering a work more *directly*. Often the *titles* they give to poems or stories or chapters in a novel are statements of how they intend us to interpret an event. The presence of the narrator in a story or poem can be even more direct than this. We especially associate such authorial intrusion with older (pre-modern) literature. For example, nineteenth-century author Nathaniel Hawthorne adds the moral "Be true" at the end of *The Scarlet Letter*. But the technique is still widely practiced. At the beginning of "Sailing to Byzantium" Irish poet and mystic William Butler Yeats declares, "That is no country for old men," and we at once know how the poet intends us to interpret the world of cyclic nature that the poem as a whole rejects.

A Case Study: "Dover Beach"

The list of ways in which writers influence an audience could go on indefinitely. But more important than a checklist of devices is simply the general alertness of a reader to the persuasive strategies of the writer. There is no formula for how a given work influences a reader. Every work is unique. To conclude my analysis of how writers influence an audience, I will use an actual example, Matthew Arnold's honeymoon poem, "Dover Beach," which one authority has called the most anthologized poem in the English language. My overriding question will be, What viewpoint does the poet try to get us to share with him, and how does he achieve that effect?

As the poem begins, someone is looking over the English Channel by night from a hotel room:

> The sea is calm tonight.
> The tide is full, the moon lies fair
> Upon the straits; on the French coast the light
> Gleams and is gone; the cliffs of England stand
> Glimmering and vast, out in the tranquil bay.
> Come to the window, sweet is the night-air!

What is the poet's strategy here? He awakens our sympathy for nature. This immediately establishes a human bond between us and the speaker. We feel "at one" with him. We see things as he sees them, and feel the peace that he feels. This human bond is strengthened when in the last line we learn that the speaker is with another person.

Through techniques of repetition and evaluative description, we experience the scene as nurturing and attractive: "calm," "full," "fair," "light," "tranquil," "sweet." Only two details stand out from the generally positive scene, and therefore function as foils. The opening line tells us that the sea is calm *tonight*. This triggers within us an awareness that on another night it might be turbulent. A similar note of uncertainty and potential transience is captured by the description of how the distant light "gleams and is gone." But these are mere ripples on an otherwise shining surface. It so happens that by the time we finish the poem we can look back on

Awakened
Sympathy for
Nature

the opening and see that these two details are much more important than we initially thought.

After the positive opening description of the scene, we are abruptly forced to see something entirely different in the scene. As we move (with the speaker, who controls what we see) from seeing to hearing, the scene suddenly becomes terrifying and threatening:

> Only, from the long line of spray
> Where the sea meets the moon-blanched land,
> Listen! you hear the grating roar
> Of pebbles which the waves draw back, and fling,
> At their return, up the high strand,
> Begin, and cease, and then again begin,
> With tremulous cadence slow, and bring
> The eternal note of sadness in.

As at the outset, we contemplate only what the poet allows us to hear. We cannot deny the threatening side of nature, because the poet has assembled the evidence right before us. Observe, therefore, how compelling is the mere presence of what a writer selects as his subject matter. Context also contributes to how we assimilate the scene: having been lulled into seeing the universe as benign, we now feel betrayed by nature and wish to protest against its destructiveness.

Subtle Persuasion

There are additional, subtle forces of influence at work in these lines. The alternating long and short lines imitate the ebb and flow of the waves and in the process draw us into the passage, placing us under its sway (such compulsion and an attendant susceptibility on the reader's part are characteristic of poetic meter wherever we find it). The very movement of the words becomes slow and melancholy in the line "Begin, and cease, and then again begin." This is reinforced by the slow moving phrase "tremulous cadence slow." In a masterful poem like this, everything contributes to the impact, and some of the effects are subconscious.

The subtle persuasion is matched by more obvious means of influence. The poet is our traveling companion, pointing out the terror of the scene with his descriptive phrase "grating roar," as well as with the verb "fling." And at the end, to clinch the point, the speaker tells us explicitly that the turbulent scene has brought "the eternal note of sadness in." This is a very evocative phrase, touching us at the deepest level of our being. As so often in literature, the writer here influences us by awakening something within us and appealing to something in our own experience. As readers we now share something very profound with the speaker, namely, an acknowledgment of the psychic pain and tragic reality that lie at the very core of our experience in the world.

Amplification

The poet's next persuasive strategy is to amplify and universalize this awareness of tragedy in life:

Sophocles long ago
Heard it on the Aegean, and it brought
Into his mind the turbid ebb and flow
Of human misery.

The ineradicable tragedy at the heart of things is more than a secret shared by poet and reader. We have now reached back through centuries of human experience to Sophocles, the Greek writer of tragedies. The fact of "human misery" has in the process been transformed from something private and local into the universal experience of the human race, perceived by its most insightful members (in whose number we as readers also stand).

The reference to Sophocles is followed by a return to the speaker on the English seacoast at Dover:

we
Find also in the sound a thought,
Hearing it by this distant northern sea.

This is mainly a transition, but even here the poet's aim is affective. Thus far the poet has been mainly descriptive as he looks at the scene. But when he now speaks of having "a thought" as he looks at the seacoast, he begins to emerge as the person of prophetic insight. Without conscious effort on our part, we have accepted the speaker's self-characterization and now await his solemn "thought." And what about the word "distant"? Distant from what? Not from the speaker, surely. A whole vision of the universe as alien and hostile is coming to dominate the poem, and even a single word like "distant" adds to the impression.

Arnold Captures the Crisis of a Whole Age

The vision of the world as hostile is elaborated in the next stanza of the poem:

The Sea of Faith
Was once, too, at the full, and round earth's shore
Lay like the folds of a bright girdle furled.
But now I only hear
Its melancholy, long, withdrawing roar,
Retreating, to the breath
Of the night-wind, down the vast edges drear
And naked shingles of the world.

Arnold here captures the crisis of a whole age. The Victorian era in England was characterized by an erosion of belief in the Christian faith. Arnold himself lost his Christian faith at college and never fully regained it. What Arnold describes in this passage is the terror of a world devoid of faith in the Christian religion.

The poet does several things to make us share his sense of despair and loneliness. He influences how we perceive the physical landscape by his descriptive terms: "melancholy, long, withdrawing roar," "vast edges drear," "naked shingles of the world." The terrifying nature of the scene is highlighted by means of a "once/now" contrast. Religious faith was "once" full and comforting. It was like a full tide and also like a bright garment tightly drawn ("furled") around a person's body, warm and secure. "Now" it is gone, leaving people exposed.

How does the poet attempt to persuade us that the Christian faith is outdated and, as he sees it, no longer tenable in the modern world? He has made the retreat of faith as tangible as the seacoast that we have been looking at since the first line of the poem. Ostensibly the poem has described only a physical landscape. But with the phrase "Sea of Faith" the reality of the physical sea becomes extended to the loss of religious faith.

Some Consolation

The beginning of the poem's last stanza springs a sudden surprise on us. The speaker addresses his companion in the room, and we learn for the first time that she is the woman whom he loves:

Ah, love, let us be true
To one another!

Here is the one place in the poem where we catch a glimpse of hope and consolation in an otherwise terrifying world. The consolation is humanistic, consisting of human love, and it is offered as a substitute for a religious faith that has disappeared. More important than the implied contrast between Christian and romantic values, however, is the fact that the consolation gets only a line and a half in the whole poem, and it is emphatically not the last word in the poem.

Two final movements in the poem quickly get our minds off the positive note of love. First the poet paints a depressing contrast between the illusory promise of happiness in the world and the actual emptiness that prevails there:

> for the world, which seems
> To lie before us like a land of dreams,
> So various, so beautiful, so new,
> Hath really neither joy, nor love, nor light,
> Nor certitude, nor peace, nor help for pain.

This is the third time in the poem where the poet has described the world positively only to undercut the description as a false delusion. As readers we have been led to share the poet's sense of betrayal. A feeling of protest begins to well up within us as the poet directs what we see and contemplate. Following the signals laid down by him, we look at the stark reality against a background of what might have been, but tragically is not, and we are angered by the failure of life to match the promise.

**A Tumultuous
Vision**

In the last three lines of the poem, the troubled vision of the speaker rises to something tumultuous. Here Arnold alludes to the Greeks' ill-fated night attack on Syracuse as recorded by Thucydides, a Greek historian from the fifth century before Christ. Using Thucydides' account as a backdrop, the poet compares life in a meaningless world to the confusion and chaos of a night battle:

> And we are here as on a darkling plain
> Swept with confused alarms of struggle and flight,
> Where ignorant armies clash by night.

Notice who is caught in this nightmare of confusion: "we are here. . . ." It is true that the speaker is addressing his beloved, but even the form of this poem (a dramatic monologue addressed to a silent listener) influences us to walk into the poem and experience the words of the speaker as directed to us.

What does Matthew Arnold wish to communicate in this poem? His aim is to get the reader to share his feeling of despair and hopelessness in a world where the Christian faith is no longer a sustaining force. Everything in the poem makes it easy for the reader to see the world from the writer's perspective. This does not mean that a reader must or should agree with the writer, and this will be my topic in the next two chapters. But we should not doubt that the influence of writers on their audience is immense.

I have chosen to speak of how "the writer" influences a reader, but all along I could have used the phrase "the work" or "the text." *Only* through their words do writers exercise their influence. Literature cannot achieve its effects at all unless we pay attention to its language and form (broadly defined). I earlier quoted David Lodge to the effect that "the writer expresses what he knows by affecting the reader; the reader knows what is expressed by being receptive to effects." Lodge's next sentence is equally crucial: "The medium of this process is language." Everything depends on the words, from which, in turn, we imagine scenes, characters, and events. The content of literature is always embodied in literary form; form itself begins with language. True, readers complete what writers begin, as I will show in the next chapter, but the writer and text always initiate and guide the communication process.

A work of literature is a highly refined system of controls.* And, writers are masters of persua-

*The most important and influential study of the rhetorical or persuasive dimension of literature continues to be Wayne Booth's book *The Rhetoric of Fiction* (Chicago: University of Chicago Press, 1961, 1983); the revised edition brings the bibliography through 1982. Also helpful are Lars Hartveit, *The Art of Persuasion: A Study of Six Novels* (Oslo: Universitetsforlaget, 1977); and Sheldon Sacks, *Fiction and the Shape of Belief* (Berkeley: University of California Press, 1964). Discussions of highlighting techniques often owe much to Axel Olrik's seminal essay, "Epic Laws of Folk Narrative," reprinted in *The Study of Folklore*, ed. Alan

**Summary:
Literature As a
Persuasive Art**

sion, though the very nature of literature can easily conceal this fact. The more artistically perfect a work is, the more effective it is in its influence. As the late Francis Schaeffer, the contemporary evangelical author and thinker, has written, "Art forms add strength to the world view which shows through, no matter what the world view is or whether the world view is true or false."[69] Similarly, Louise Rosenblatt, a current literary theorist, argues that the values embodied in literature "are reinforced by the persuasiveness of art."[70] The power of literature to persuade, for good or bad, lies behind Romantic poet Percy Bysshe Shelley's famous statement that "poets are the unacknowledged legislators of the world."[71]

Critics and Teachers of Literature Have a Bias, Too

I am going to emphasize my next comment because it is so often overlooked. If writers of literature influence an audience, *so do critics and teachers of literature.* Critics and teachers also have biases. The commentary that literature teachers give in the classroom is far from objective. Even the authors and works that a teacher/critic selects for attention reflect his or her own interests and outlook. Furthermore, what a teacher/critic then decides to stress in a work of literature is influenced by his or her temperament and bias.

In fact, critics exercise persuasion in approximately the same ways that writers do. They

Dundes (Englewood Cliffs: Prentice-Hall, 1965), pp. 131–41. On the presence of the writer in a text, see Geoffrey Tillotson, "Authorial Presence: Some Observations," in *Imagined Worlds,* ed. Maynard Mack and Ian Gregor (London: Methuen, 1968), pp. 215–23. Still useful are the introductory essay, explications, and bibliography in *Rhetorical Analyses of Literary Works,* ed. Edward P. J. Corbett (New York: Oxford University Press, 1969). A more advanced study is that by Seymour Chatman, *Story and Discourse: Narrative Structure in Fiction and Film* (Ithaca: Cornell University Press, 1978).

stress some aspects of a work and ignore other aspects. They either include or omit critical viewpoints that disagree with their own. They choose sides in regard to characters and events in a work. They make direct interpretive statements about works. They can easily suppress certain aspects of a work and exaggerate others. They also create an atmosphere that can influence an audience. I have a colleague who was the first student ever to raise a hand in the experience of a professor who, whenever he taught Hawthorne's *The Scarlet Letter,* asked if there was anyone in the class who thought adultery was wrong.

It is a truism that we are often most influenced when we don't realize that we are being subjected to persuasive strategies. Critics and teachers of literature have subtle but immense influence on how readers view works of literature. Interpretations of literary works shift drastically through the years. The Christian faith gets a better hearing in literature courses on secular campuses than in most other courses because so much of the older literature was rooted in the Christian faith. Yet the prevailing biases in literary criticism are secularistic rather than religious. They are based on a hedonistic ethic that rejects Christian moral restraints, especially in sexual matters. The prevailing spirit of literary criticism is naturalistic to the exclusion of the supernatural. And it tends to have an evolutionary view of man as a bundle of conditioned drives and reflexes.

What this means is that students of literature have to be discerning when they listen to a teacher or read criticism. Readers have a right to reach their own conclusions about works of literature. They are not obliged to see only what a teacher/critic points out, no matter how brilliant that person may be.

104

Windows
to the
World

The
Persuasiveness
of Literature:
Friend or Foe?

The Christian tradition has never been able to make up its mind on the question of whether the persuasiveness of literature is good or bad. Much has been said on both sides.

As far back as Augustine, the persuasiveness of literature has been regarded as fearsome and a good reason for staying away from literature, especially drama. After Augustine became a Christian, he looked back in revulsion at how his emotional life had been manipulated by the dramatic performances he had attended in his younger years. Augustine concluded that literature infected people with unwholesome emotions and led them into immoral behavior. He also worried about the intellectual influence of literature. He believed that literature is instructive but suspect because it teaches error rather than truth.[72]

The Renaissance poet Sir Philip Sidney looked at the ability of literature to move a reader and came to the opposite conclusion. Sidney theorized that the persuasiveness of literature makes it ideally suited to moving readers "from wickedness to virtue." This ability of literature to move a reader to virtuous behavior was sufficient to make Sidney regard it as the most important of all the disciplines, better even than history and philosophy.[73]

Between these poles, Christians have argued about whether literature is friend or foe. The truth is that it is both.

The Potential Dangers of Literature's Persuasiveness

Why would Christians fear the affective power of literature? Christians have standards of truth and morality that they regard as absolute. From this presupposition, they have objections to what happens when the persuasiveness of literature influences people away from truth and morality.

The potential dangers fall into several categories. Literature can persuade a reader to accept an erroneous viewpoint as the truth. It can move a person to detrimental emotions, such as the despair that so much modern literature induces. And it has the potential to influence a person to immoral behavior.

These dangers are not simply hypothetical. Anyone who reads much literature or attends movies has probably experienced all of them. No less a literary giant than C. S. Lewis commented, "I could not doubt that the sub-Christian or anti-Christian values implicit in most literature did actually infect many readers."[74]

The affective nature of literature means that Christian readers cannot afford to be naive about what happens when they read a story or poem or attend a play. Reading literature should not be the occasion for letting down one's guard. The persuasiveness of literature is not a reason to avoid literature, but it is a challenge to be an alert reader. We cannot afford to stop thinking when we sit down to read a book or attend a play.

This applies also to recreational reading. T. S. Eliot has sounded this caution in his great essay "Religion and Literature":

> I incline to come to the alarming conclusion that it is just the literature that we read for "amusement," or "purely for pleasure" that may have the greatest and least suspected influence upon us. It is the literature which we read with the least effort that can have the easiest and most insidious influence upon us.[75]

The very eloquence and technical skill of great authors can make us hesitate to disagree with them. But as readers and as Christians we should not be intimidated by great writers. *Their skill with the craft of literature does not guarantee the truthfulness of their viewpoint.* Francis Schaeffer is right when he states,

> As Christians, we must see that just because an artist—even a great artist—portrays a world view in writing or on canvas, it does not mean that we

should automatically accept that world view. . . .
The truth of a world view presented by an artist
must be judged on grounds other than artistic
greatness.[76]

Before leaving the topic of the potential for
literature to influence a person in negative ways,
I need to add that this danger is not limited to
literature. Advertising and the news media also
manipulate and mislead people. Christian students can have their faith undermined in a
psychology or history or religion course as well
as in a literature course. And if the emotional
impact of literature is taken to be inherently
harmful, we will also have to cancel our football
and basketball games, to say nothing of our
hymn-sings and political campaigns.

**The Potential
for Good**

If the influence of literature is potentially bad,
it is also potentially good. Christians should not
doubt this, for the Bible itself displays all of the
persuasive strategies of literature that I discussed earlier in this chapter, and many more
besides. Christians do not avoid other areas of
life simply because a possibility for abuse exists.
By the same logic, they should not neglect
literature, as they sometimes have, simply because it can be abused. If literature contains
much that is untrue, it also contains much that is
true.

Skill in craftsmanship and beauty of expression gain a sympathetic hearing from readers
who would otherwise reject a writer's viewpoint
out of hand. Because so much literature has
been rooted in the Christian faith, the study of
literature in a secular setting can be a positive
thing for the Christian faith. I continue to be
thrilled that such obviously Christian poets as
George Herbert and John Milton and Gerard
Manley Hopkins receive such positive treatment
by teachers and critics of literature on the
strength of their literary excellence. If literature

can make error appealing, it can also make Christian truth appealing. Contemporary British author, editor, and humorist Malcolm Muggeridge has written that "books like *Resurrection* and *The Brothers Karamazov* give me an almost overpowering sense of how uniquely marvelous a Christian way of looking at life is, and a passionate desire to share it."[77]

For the Christian who has a talent for writing literature, the affective nature of literature is an open door to having a positive influence in society. The power of literature both to reveal the truth and to touch people at the deepest level makes literature an ally in the war of truth and in the battle to capture people's hearts and minds.

If you are a Christian writer, I would urge you to take seriously the principle that the power of literature resides in its artistic excellence. There is a difference between literature and propaganda. Good literature is artistically proficient, incarnational rather than abstract, subtle or indirect rather than overly direct in its approach to truth. Writers and film makers who respect the nature of literature produce a lasting effect on the Christian world, and enjoy an entry into the secular world, that propagandistic writers do not.

In considering the affective power of literature, we should think also of the entertainment side of literature, not just its concern with ideas and viewpoints. The ability of literature to captivate an audience has as much to do with form as with content. The spell that a gripping story puts on us, or the admiration that is elicited by a great sonnet, or the ability of a description to move us, is an essential part of the total effectiveness of literature.

Nor do I share the aversion of Plato and Augustine to the emotional side of literature. The emotional states that literature can produce in individuals and societies often produce beneficial psychic results. Furthermore, people's emotions are no more depraved than their minds are. The Romantic poets have a lot to teach us about the positive side of the emotional nature of literature. Our emotions, as well as our minds, need direction and nurture. Shelley claimed that with the right kind of literature "the good affections are strengthened," and Wordsworth believed that such literature causes readers to find their "affections strengthened and purified."[78]

Respecting the Rights of an Author

This chapter has been an implied defense of the role of writers in the literary enterprise. We should welcome the presence of writers in their works. I believe, moreover, that writers have a moral right not to have their work misinterpreted. This means that readers have an obligation to allow writers to govern the interpretation of works of literature, at least in the measure to which the writers have provided the necessary guidelines. As readers, we can always exercise our prerogative of disagreeing with what has been written. But we do not have a right to twist a writer's work in such a way that it ends up meaning something contrary to what the writer intended. Given a choice of interpretations, we should make whatever use we can of a writer's intention (to the extent that we know it).

This means that Christian readers will necessarily distance themselves from certain extreme forms of reader-centered criticism. The most extreme form is known as "deconstruction." It is based on the premise that works of literature do not possess meaning and that therefore readers are free to "deconstruct" a work and create their own meanings in place of the text. This is an affront to the writer and a violation of a common human right, namely, that our utterances be interpreted in keeping with what we say and mean. The intentional or biographical approach to literature is already enjoying a revival as a reaction against some forms of reader-centered criticism.*

SUMMARY

Writers compose and publish works of literature because they wish to communicate with an audience. In keeping with the nature of literary form, writers are able to exploit a whole range of rhetorical techniques in order to influence the thoughts and feelings and interpretations of their audience. This persuasive element in literature requires that readers not only be alert but also respect the writer's side of the literary transaction.

---

*Anyone wishing to defend the right of authors to determine how their work is interpreted will find assistance in the following sources: D. Newton-de Molina, ed., *On Literary Intention* (Edinburgh: Edinburgh University Press, 1976); E. D. Hirsch, Jr., *Validity in Interpretation* (New Haven: Yale University Press, 1967); Peter D. Juhl, *Interpretation: An Essay in the Philosophy of Literary Criticism* (Princeton: Princeton University Press, 1980). The first source is the best starting point and contains further bibliographic suggestions.

chapter five

How Readers Complete What Writers Begin

Reading is a complex endeavor involving both what the literature brings to us and what we bring to it. Good readers are always active: interpreting, evaluating, and analyzing. They also are constantly aware of their own responses to what they read.

The process of communication described in the previous chapter requires an audience to complete it. A work of literature ultimately exists only if the reader has transformed the words on the page into a personal experience. Consequently, what readers get out of a work of literature depends largely upon what they bring to it.

**What Readers
Contribute to
Literature**

A recent trend that is highly significant is the increasing influence of the reader-centered approach to literature, also called reader-response criticism.* The approach is based on a truism that the words on a page have no real meaning or impact until a reader does something with them. Chapter 4 suggested that in a sense, readers are totally dependent on a writer, that is, on what a writer puts before them. But, likewise, writers depend on readers to complete the literary process that writers begin.

The fact that the work itself is the starting point for whatever happens when we read can easily convey the illusion that all of the input is coming from the writer's side, via the text. But the words are only a potential. Unless the reader fills those words with content, no literary process occurs. The literary work depends on the *reader's response* to the words, images, and characters that a writer puts into a work. French philosopher Jean-Paul Sartre has written,

> Since the artist must entrust to another the job of carrying out what he has begun, since it is only through the consciousness of the reader that he can regard himself as essential to his work, . . . the writer appeals to the reader's freedom to collaborate in the production of his work.[79]

Even the simplest literature involves the participation of a reader. Note Milton's description of Paradise (*Paradise Lost*, book 4):

---

*The best single book on the role of the reader in the literary experience is by Louise M. Rosenblatt, *The Reader, the Text, the Poem: The Transactional Theory of the Literary Work* (Carbondale: Southern Illinois University Press, 1978). A good starting point for mastering the overall movement is the following two anthologies of essays: *The Reader in the Text: Essays on Audience and Interpretation*, ed. Susan R. Suleiman and Inge Crosman (Princeton: Princeton University Press, 1980); and *Reader-Response Criticism: From Formalism to Post-Structuralism*, ed. Jane P. Tompkins (Baltimore: Johns Hopkins University Press, 1980). Both books contain full, annotated bibliographies on the subject. In forging my own theory of how the reader participates in literature, I benefited most from Simon O. Lesser, *Fiction and the Unconscious* (Chicago: University of Chicago Press, 1957; reprint, 1975).

a circling row
Of goodliest trees loaden with fairest fruit,
Blossoms and fruits at once of golden hue.

Milton's words are only an outline. They stimulate readers to fill in the outline on the basis of their own experience. Exactly what are these "goodliest trees" and "fairest fruit"? They are whatever a given reader's imagination supplies to the words. No wonder literary scholars today speak of the reader's "answering imagination" as a necessary part of literature. Literature is like a meal: the cook (the author) brings the food (the words) and the guest (the reader) partakes, completing the meal (meaning).

When readers supply meaning in this way, they obviously do so in terms of their own background and experiences. How you assimilate a love story or a poem about death depends on your experiences (or lack of them) with love and death. Related to this is the so-called inexhaustability of a work of literature. The same work of literature keeps meaning more and different things to the same reader over a span of time because our experience of life keeps expanding. Sartre said regarding a reader that "the work exists only at the exact level of his capacities; while he reads and creates, he knows that he can always go further in his reading, can always create more profoundly."[80]

The common way of describing the activity of the reader is what literary scholars call "the hermeneutical circle" ("interpretive circle"). We can diagram it this way:

reader's experience   work of literature

What the diagram means is this: our responses to literature are rooted in our experiences in real life. We bring our background of experiences and beliefs *to* the story or poem. But we also reverse that process. In the experiences of life we are reminded of the stories and characters and scenes and lines of poetry with which we are familiar. We carry literature to life and use it to organize and illuminate our experiences.

To be good readers, we need to know what types of activities we are required to perform as we read. In the theory of reading that follows, I have organized the material into six main headings. Together these describe what happens when we do our job well as readers.

Reading With Imagination

In the first place, good readers exercise their *imagination*. Modern literary theory has championed the role of the imagination in literature, but it has unjustifiably limited the discussion to writers. A little reflection will show, however, that the functions we ascribe to the imagination apply to the reader as well as to the writer.

Imagination, for example, means the ability to experience images—concrete sensory phenomena. The Russian fiction writer Nabokov has written, "In reading, one should notice and fondle details. . . . We must see things and hear things, we must visualize the rooms, the clothes, the manners of an author's people."[81] The most significant breakthrough in my recent literary experience came when I started using slide presentations in my teaching of literature. The more visual we are as readers, the richer will be our literary experience.

Imagination also implies creativity—the ability to produce something new from one's own resources. It is an activity that the reader performs as well as the writer. Once again, Sartre has expressed it well: "Reading is directed creation. . . . The author's whole art is bent on obliging me to *create* what he *discloses*."[82] Good reading is not a spectator sport. It occurs when readers are fully active—active in picturing details, seeing patterns, contributing meanings to words, finding connections among the parts of the work, entering into the "world" of a work and going through the events with the characters in a story or the speaker in a lyric poem.

Readers do not, of course, create out of nothing. But then neither do writers. Both work with the materials at hand, the writer with real life, the reader with the words and images of the work, which are in turn related to the experiences of real life. Readers use the words of a text to produce the final work. To disregard the limits that a text places on a reader's creativity is an affront to a writer; but not to be a creative reader is just as defeating to a writer.

Another key element in any theory of what happens when we read is summed up in the word *encounter*. When we sit down to read a story or poem, we are asking for an encounter. What, specifically, do we encounter?

Reading As Encounter

We encounter people—characters in a story, the speaker in a lyric poem, the narrator in a story, and the author of the work. We also encounter human experience—love, death, nature, human emotions, and, taking literature as a whole, the entire range of human experience. We encounter the physical world and the moral/spiritual world in which we live; this world includes nature, the world of external objects, the moral world of good and evil, the spiritual world of God and angels and heaven and hell. We encounter ideas, as expressed by characters within a work and as embodied in the work as a whole. And we encounter the artistic side of literature—the beauty, the form, the artistry.

If reading literature is this type of encounter, the corollary that follows is that as readers we must be prepared to meet a work of literature half way. We need to be alert, as we are when we meet a person of note or attend an event of importance. We must not be passive readers. We must stand up, as it were, and engage in an ongoing dialogue—an active give and take—as we read a piece of literature. Any successful encounter depends on the interaction of the two persons engaged in the encounter. Reading literature is no different.

Reading As Discovery

A good theory of reading also includes the idea of *discovery*. When we start to read a work of literature, we embark on a process of discovering what the work stands ready to reveal.

In reading literature we discover insights about human experience, not necessarily new insights, since they might be reminders of insights that are old to us. One of the tasks of the writer is that of revelation—revelation about life and the world. Shelley said that the poet "withdraws life's dark veil from before the scene of things."[83] Robert Frost was getting at the same thing when he described the writing of a poem as a process in which he experienced "the surprise of remembering something I didn't know I knew. . . . There is a glad recognition of the long-lost."[84] The same type of discovery belongs to the reader. As readers we discover the properties of the work itself—how it is made, how the parts fit together, how one or more overriding themes unify the work, how the writer is leading us through an experience.

In the creative act of composing a work, writers gradually discover and arrange the details and final shape of the work. Readers do something very similar as they creatively "stare" at a work. Someone has written that

the critic is interested, like the artist, in technique, . . . in structure, the aesthetic properties of the thing made, its architectonic features such as unity, balance, emphasis, rhythm, and . . . the shapely pattern resulting when all the materials . . . have been brought into more or less complete interplay and fullness of tension. When the whole work finally springs to life in his mind, the critic experiences a delight, a joy in the thing of beauty, akin to that of the artist when his vision at length fell into shape.[85]

To scrutinize a literary work closely is a creative act, and it allows a reader to make many of the same discoveries that the author made while composing the work.

What are the implications of looking upon the act of reading as a process of discovery? Primarily it imposes on the reader the obligation to be perceptive, to be creative, to be active in looking. Flannery O'Connor's advice that writers "should never be ashamed of staring" applies equally to readers.[86] People who love literature are the ones who look upon every reading experience as an adventure. They approach reading with the openness, the receptivity, the curiosity, the expectancy that characterize every true explorer.

Reading As Recognition

When we read literature we not only open ourselves up to an encounter and a process of discovery. We also experience something that I will call *recognition*. At the level of subject matter, literature gives us forms for our own experiences, feelings, and beliefs. The writer expresses our own experiences, our own impulses and fears, some of them hidden or repressed, in the form of a story or poem or play.

We spend most of our lives only vaguely aware of the inner flow of our mind and emotions ar ' impulses. When we read literature, what is unconscious or chaotic within us becomes projected onto characters in a play or landscapes in a story or images in a poem. In the process, we recognize the feelings and impulses and experiences and memories that lie within us. Impulses toward courage or heroism or love or security, to name just a few, are objictified for us. This is what was meant by Emerson when he called the writer "the namer" and by Sartre when he commented that through words a writer "shapes our feelings, names them, and attributes them to an imaginary personage who takes it upon himself to live them for us and who has no other substance than these borrowed passions".[87] Simon Lesser, a twentieth-century literary critic, puts it this way: "Fiction *objectifies* our problems: it translates what was internal and amorphous, or too close to us to be seen clearly, into something outside ourselves and easy to perceive."[88]

When writers thus give shape to common human experience, readers, for their part, undergo a process of recognition. Dorothy Sayers theorizes that in the writer's experience

> we can *recognise* . . . some experience of our own—something that had happened to us, but which we had never understood, never formulated or expressed to ourselves. . . . When we read the poem, or see the play or picture or hear the music, it is as though a light were turned on us. We say: "Ah! I recognise that! That is something which I obscurely felt to be going on in and about me, but I didn't know what it was and couldn't express it. But now that the artist has . . . imaged it forth . . . for me, I can possess and take hold of it and make it my own, and turn it into a source of knowledge and strength."[89]

The two big subjects of literature are human fears and longings (recall the two columns of archetypes on the chart on pp. 46-48). In reading literature, we recognize our own fears and longings, our own nightmares and dreams. One good question to ask as we read, therefore, is, What longings or desires and what fears or anxieties that I myself feel are awakened and given shape as I read this work of literature? An additional thing to note is that, as Simon Lesser says, the literature that elicits the strongest response from us is literature that presents "experiences we would like to have or fear we may have to endure."[90]

In order to insure the relevance of literature to our life, we need to be active in "building bridges" between a work of literature and our own experiences. Great literature, even though it presents characters and actions and settings remote from us, uses those particulars to present universal human experience, including our own. The approach of literature to truth is always through the particular, the concrete, the specific character or setting or event. But these particulars are a net to capture the universal element in human experience.

If the particulars of literature capture the universal, the task of the reader is to transform that universal into something specific in his own life and culture. At the level of issues or experiences, it is always possible to walk into a work of literature and make it our own, and this is something we must do if our reading is going to be relevant. We might diagram the process like this:

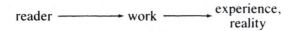

reader ⟶ work ⟶ experience, reality

As readers, we not only look *at* the work but also *through* it to our own experience in the world. It is the task of readers to recognize their own experiences in the details of a work, no matter how remote those details may appear to be on the surface. Aldous Huxley once wrote, "One of our most ordinary reactions to a good piece of literary art is expressed in the formula: 'This is what I always felt and thought, but have never been able to put clearly into words, even for myself.' "[91]

Walker Percy, the contemporary novelist from Louisiana, said something similar:

The purpose of art is to transmit universal truths. . . . In art, whether it's poetry, fiction or painting, you are telling the reader or the listener something he already knows but which he doesn't quite know that he knows, so that in the action of communication he experiences a recognition, a feeling that he has been there before, a shock of recognition. And so, what the artist does . . . is simply to validate the human experience and to tell people the deep human truths which they already unconsciously know.[92]

Reading As Self-Revelation

Another word that summarizes what happens when we read is *self-revelation*. On a superficial view, readers judge works of literature. As they read and ponder, they decide to their own satisfaction if the work is well or poorly written, interesting or dull, if the writer's viewpoint is right or wrong, if characters and events in the work are sympathetic or unsympathetic.

But if readers judge works of literature, the reverse is also true. Contemporary literary theorist Stanley Fish has written that "books (sacred and profane) read the reader. . . . Books draw out what is in a man."[93] In other words, our responses as we read literature are *self*-revealing. Our literary responses are an index to what we believe, feel, have experienced, and so forth. For the reading of literature to be fully beneficial, therefore, we need to ponder our judgments and responses as we read. We need to notice the types of fictional characters and events that we identify with strongly, and what types repel us.

Reading can make us more self-aware and self-critical. It can be a way of discovering things about ourselves, especially about our values and morality. We should pay particular attention to the types of literature to which we gravitate when left to our own tastes, or the works that elicit the strongest feelings from us. Simon Lesser theorizes that "we read primarily to discover ourself—above all, perhaps, to discover what St. Augustine refers to as the dark corners of the heart."[94] (I assume that "dark" here means "hidden, subconscious.") Perhaps the clearest example on record of how a response to literature can lead to self-revelation and self-awareness is the response of King David to Nathan's fictional parable (2 Sam. 12:1–15). In condemning a character in the story, David was really making a judgment against himself. Our responses as readers of literature are not always that dramatic, but they always become the occasion by which we reveal something about ourselves.

A final activity that readers perform is *interpretation*. To interpret literature is to make a statement regarding what it *means*. Most readers do not realize how continuously they engage in such interpretations. From the smallest detail to the overall meaning of a work, literature places the task of interpretation on its readers.

Consider such a small element of literature as a metaphor or simile. A metaphor or simile is an implied comparison between two things. A famous simile in modern poetry occurs at the beginning of T. S. Eliot's poem "The Love Song of J. Alfred Prufrock," where Eliot compares the evening to "a patient etherized upon a table." A poetic comparison like this always requires a reader to interpret exactly *how* one half is like the other half. The poet does not tell us how an evening is like a patient on an operating table. He entrusts to readers the task of interpretation, inviting readers to discover the meaning for themselves.

Stories place similar demands on readers. One of the commonest things we do with stories might be called "choosing a hero." As we encounter characters in a story, we inevitably respond to them with sympathy, indifference, or antipathy. We respond with similar judgments to the actions that characters undertake in a story.

To respond to characters and actions this way is to make a decision about the meaning of the story.

Once we acknowledge that readers are always busy making big and small interpretations as they read, we also have to notice that they do not agree in their interpretations. They disagree about literature partly because they respond to literature in terms of their own experiences and beliefs. (I say "partly" because some readers simply do a better job than others of paying attention to the details in the work of literature.) It was exactly this variability of interpretations that produced current reader-response criticism.

We should note in passing that the variability of interpretations proves that writers cannot fully control a reader's response to their works. No literary effects are automatic. Despite all the means of persuasion that I noted in the previous chapter, writers are, in the last resort, at the mercy of their readers.

For example, the Russian novelist Fyodor Dostoyevsky wrote a novel (*The Brothers Karamazov*) in which he portrays at great length the lives of a father and his sons. The father is a completely carnal person. One son is a learned atheist, another is a Christian, and a third is torn apart by an inner conflict between grace and carnality.

Which of these is the hero with whom we most closely identify and whom we admire? The narrator in the story makes every effort to generate sympathy for the Christian, named Alyosha. He calls him "my hero." He begins and ends the story with him. He portrays Alyosha as an idealized figure liked by everyone else in the story. But as scholars and readers talk about the novel, it becomes obvious that they do not all gravitate toward the Christian in the story. Some readers resonate with the unbelieving brother, others with the tortured Dmitri and his conflicting impulses. Why don't readers agree? Because they interpret the story in light of their own experiences and values.

Or consider the following poem by contemporary poet and playwright E. E. Cummings:

in Just-
spring   when the world is mud-
luscious the little
lame balloonman

whistles   far   and wee

and eddieandbill come
running from marbles and
piracies and it's
spring

when the world is puddle-wonderful

the queer
old balloonman whistles
far   and   wee
and bettyandisbel come dancing

from hop-scotch and jump-rope and

it's
spring
and
   the

      goat-footed

balloonMan   whistles
far
and
wee

A romanticist in the mode of Wordsworth and Whitman will look at the poem and read it as a happy springtime poem. After all, it is filled with images of nature and children, both of them positive norms for a romanticist. How could a poem with phrases like "mud-luscious" and "puddle-wonderful" be anything other than a celebration of spring and childhood? It is no wonder that the poem appears on school bulletin boards when spring rolls around. And as for the fact that the balloonman is goatfooted, a touch of myth is always welcome to a romanticist.

A pessimistic naturalist in the mode of Thomas Hardy will see something far more sinister in the poem. Such a reader will observe that a common pattern occurs three times: children are led away from their games (which include piracies as well as marbles, incidentally) by an old balloonman. Such a reader will point out, moreover, that the key to the poem's meaning is the progressive characterization of the balloonman. As the poem unfolds, these adjectives are attached to the balloonman: little, lame, queer, old, goat-footed. This is an increasingly negative portrait. The goat-footed balloonman turns out to be a figure from classical mythology—the lustful satyr or faun, half animal and half man. In classical mythology the satyrs and fauns are associated with sensuality, and some of the stories are about their seduction of nymphs in a forest setting. Far from being a vision of innocence, the poem, says the pessimistic naturalist, is a comment about the essentially animalistic nature of humankind. What else can we expect from a creature who evolved from predatory animals?

Christian readers, in turn, will see something additional in the poem. In the picture of children being led from childhood to evil adulthood, they are reminded of what their theology calls the Fall—the Fall from original innocence into sin as narrated in Genesis 3. They would also make something of the fact that there are only two words capitalized in the poem, "Just" and "Man." The balloonman is "just man"—the representative of essential humanity. Human nature is inherently evil, according to the poem. There are, however, hints of an alternative to that evil, both within the poem and in Christian doctrine. Evil is not humankind's initial state; it is a pathological condition, brought upon the human race by Adam's sin in the Garden and by people's own choices. A Christian reader, remembering Christ's words about the sheep and the goats, might also see the balloonman as a demonic figure (in Christian iconography, the devil is sometimes pictured as having goat's feet).

What does it all add up to? That readers partly see in the poem what their framework of beliefs and presuppositions equips them to see.

Having emphasized the subjective element in reading, I must urge a caution. Readers do not have a right to make a work say anything they wish to see in the work. Any legitimate response to a work must be a response to something that is really there. The words on the page set certain boundaries to the meanings that can be ascribed to a work.

The Text As the Final Authority

That is why Northrop Frye writes that a "right" interpretation of a work is the one "that conforms to the intentionality of the book itself and to the conventions it assumes and requires."[95] Even the most thoroughgoing reader-response critics agree that the text exercises control over a reader's responses. One of them writes,

> If communication between text and reader is to be successful, clearly the reader's activity must also be controlled in some way by the text. . . . The guiding devices operative in the reading process have to initiate communication and to control it.[96]

Reader-response criticism has immense implications for Christian readers. Simply put, it opens the door for them to be themselves when they read literature. Christian readers need not apologize for having a value system and for having an "agenda" of interests. *All* readers approach literature with their own background of experiences and values.

Christians As Readers: The New Freedom

When a literary critic wrote the following

passage in 1959, it was a mildly shocking claim, even to Christians:

> Of course, it is the whole person who responds to a poem or novel; and if that person is a believing Christian, then it is a believing Christian who judges; one can't . . . pretend to be something one is not. . . . Literary criticism is as much a personal matter, as much the product of a personal sense of life and value as literature itself.[97]

Today this claim is not charged with controversy. The whole climate of literary theory today makes it seem familiar.

Reader-response theory has produced the best opportunity in recent history for Christian readers/critics to get a fair hearing in the academic world. Christians are not asking for a privilege that others do not also expect, namely, the right to respond to literature in terms of who they really are.

This is not to say that non-Christians will not continue to show hostility to Christians. A feature of college life that is still common on secular campuses is English professors who ask Christian students in a class to identify themselves and then proceed to belittle their ability to study literature. When professors do this, of course, they are doing something that has nothing to do with literature and everything to do with their own hostility to Christianity. They will not be silenced by *literary* arguments, but they can at least be challenged by the following literary statements, which come from four leading literary theorists on the scene today:

> Each reader brings to the [literary] transaction not only a specific past life and literary history . . . , but also a very active present, with all its preoccupations, anxieties, questions and aspirations. . . . The reader's response is regulated . . . not only by the incidence of elements in the text but also by what he brings to it.[98]

> There can be no "presuppositionless" interpretation. A biblical, literary, or scientific text is not

interpreted without preconceptions. . . . Where do we get our presuppositions? From the tradition in which we stand.[99]

Reading is a wholly subjective process and . . . the nature of what is perceived is determined by. . . the personality of the perceiver. . . . The role of personality in response is the most fundamental fact of criticism.[100]

. . . every reading of a text always takes place within a community, a tradition, or a living current of thought, all of which display presuppositions and exigencies—regardless of how closely a reading may be tied to . . . the text.[101]

What all of these statements share is a conviction that readers of literature assimilate literature through the "filter" of their own world view. It is only a logical extension of this principle when a Christian critic writes,

A Christian . . . will see life in Christian terms. . . . And the non-Christian critic—let us be clear about this—will also judge a writer's insight into character (or into anything else, of course) by the standard of his own insight, however derived. There is . . . no critical neutrality.[102]

Everyone sees literature through his or her reservoir of life experiences and world view. The following diagram applies equally to Christians and any other readers:

reader ⟶ reader's experiences and beliefs ⟶ work of literature

We all look at stories and poems through the "lens" of our own system of beliefs and experiences and previous acquaintance with literature.

The current state of literary theory, with its emphasis on "interpretive communities," has provided a place for Christian readers to stand. Christians *are* an interpretive community. They have their own agenda of interests and their own set of mental and emotional "antennae." As such, they are entirely normal.

Christians As Readers: The Responsibilities

With the new freedom naturally come responsibilities. Christian readers, as well as others, need first of all to let writers and their works say what they really mean. Reading should follow a two-stage process. In the first stage, a reader tries to let the author and work assert their own meanings. In the second stage, readers fit those assertions into their own system of beliefs. In keeping with a writer's right not to have his or her literary statements twisted to say something other than what the author intended, readers should make every effort to resist making a work say what they themselves believe. The persuasive strategies that the writer builds into a work function as guideposts that readers should respect.

Furthermore, if it is true that Christian readers respond to literature as Christians, we should also remember that they do not respond *only* as Christians. They are also members of the human race at large and therefore respond to literature simply as humans. Literature is one of the great humanizing agencies in culture. Christians have every reason to welcome literature as an entry into the human community.

Christians also need to extend to others the same rights of readership that they expect as an interpretive community. This will without doubt involve toleration of what will seem obvious misreadings of works of literature. It will mean entering into charitable dialogue with people who disregard the Christian element in works of literature (a parallel to the misunderstandings that people show in regard to the Bible).

Along with the gains of reader-centered criticism have come some losses. To the extent to which we impose our own viewpoints on works of literature, we relinquish the self-forgetfulness

that is one of the chief rewards of reading.
Furthermore, when we see in literature only
what we bring to it, we cut off the possibility of
expanding ourselves, which is also a leading
reward of reading. C. S. Lewis has championed
a view of literature that sees its value in its
ability to get us beyond ourselves and allow us
to see the world through someone else's eyes.
He writes,

> We demand windows. Literature . . . is a series of
> windows, even of doors. One of the things we feel
> after reading a great work is "I have got out". . . .
> The primary impulse of each is to maintain and
> aggrandise himself. The secondary impulse is to go
> out of the self, to correct its provincialism. . . .
> Obviously this process can be described either as
> an enlargement or as a temporary annihilation of
> the self. . . . The man who is contented to be only
> himself . . . is in prison. My own eyes are not
> enough for me, I will see through those of
> others.[103]

This is a value of reading literature that I am
not willing to surrender, and it is at odds with
the idea that we should be self-conscious about
ourselves as we read literature. We cannot be
self-forgetful and self-conscious at the same
time. The only resolution that I have come up
with is to recognize that reading is a complex
activity. Part of the time we can forget ourselves
and follow the advice of Lewis that "the first
demand any work of art makes upon us is
surrender. Look. Listen. Receive. Get yourself
out of the way."[104] At other times we are
reflective readers, self-conscious about how our
own personality and beliefs enter into our total
literary response. Often the two activities fall
into a two-stage process: during the actual act of
reading we forget ourselves, but as we subse-
quently make sense of what we have read, we do
so within the context of our personality and
world view.

SUMMARY

The art of reading demands an active reader. To read well, and to enjoy reading literature on our own initiative, we need to exercise our imagination, and to read with a sense of encounter, discovery, and recognition. We should also scrutinize our responses to literature to see what those responses reveal about our own attitudes and values.

Readers are also active in interpreting what they read. They are continuously required to make decisions about what the details in a story or poem mean. In making such interpretations, readers are influenced by their own background of experiences and beliefs. For Christian readers, this means reading in the light of Christian experience and a Christian world view.

chapter six

Does Literature Tell the Truth?

Works of literature embody a world view—a set of basic premises about reality, values, and morality. Any complete analysis of literature includes discovering the contours of a work's world view and then comparing it to one's own.

As previous chapters have shown, literature serves many functions. It is an art form. It is a type of recreation. It is a picture of human experience that enables us to understand life better.

All of these have value in themselves, but they do not tell the whole story. When writers put pen to paper, they intend their story or play or poem to be a truthful comment about reality. Writers, like all of us, have a vision of how things are or should be. In telling their story or

Literature's Claim to Truth

131

writing their poem, they try to get readers to see things their way. In short, works of literature possess meaning. They make implied claims to truth and need to be assessed in such a way (though not to the neglect of other ways).

A little reflection will show why literature cannot avoid meaning something and making assertions about reality. The subject of literature is human experience; as a result, "the primary convention of literature" (to quote Jonathan Culler, a modern literary theorist) is "the rule of significance: read the [work] as expressing a significant attitude to some problem concerning man and/or his relation to the universe."[105] Someone else notes that "since literature involves the whole range of human concerns, it is impossible to avoid assuming some attitude toward them."[106]

Works of literature are not pointless. The last thing in the world that a writer wishes a reader to ask at the end of a story or poem is, "So what?" Writers consequently take pains to assure a reader, however subtly, that they are making a comment about significant aspects of human experience. When Southern novelist and short story writer William Faulkner accepted the Nobel Prize for Literature in 1949, he said that the writer's duty is to write about the human soul,

> a spirit capable of compassion and sacrifice and endurance. . . . It is his privilege to help man endure by lifting his head. . . . The poet's voice need not merely be the record of man, it can be one of the props, the pillars to help him endure and prevail.[107]

This is a very high goal for literature, perhaps higher than literature as a whole has achieved, but it dispels any doubt that writers intend to make a significant comment about life. In refreshing contrast to many modern critics who are not content until they have reduced literature to so many ambiguities that it ceases to say anything at all, novelist Joyce Cary has said that it is the responsibility of a writer to insure that "a reader . . . never be left in doubt about the meaning of a story."[108]

Writers even choose stories and situations on the basis of their significance and ability to embody truth. Storytellers, for example, are always on the lookout for "good stories" and strong plots, but they have another criterion as well. They choose stories in which—to use the words of Baudelaire, the nineteenth-century French poet—"the deep significance of life reveals itself."[109]

Literature does more than *present* human experience; it also interprets experience. It offers a perspective on whatever topic the writer selects. Shakespeare's *Macbeth* does more than *portray* the hero's excessive ambition; it also condemns such ambition as a moral evil. T. S. Eliot is not content to narrate what happened to J. Alfred Prufrock on the way to a tea party; he uses the situation to express the sense of emptiness and lack of values of people in the modern world. In short, literature embodies attitudes toward the world and offers these implied statements as truth.

That an author intends a meaning is one of the interpretive assumptions with which we approach literature. If we saw words scrawled on a rocky cliff, we would try to determine their meaning on the assumption that someone wrote them there for a purpose. If, however, we learned that the markings were caused by erosion, we would not try to get a meaning from them. Works of literature are obviously not caused by erosion but are part of an author's intention.*

---

*The current emphasis in literary criticism on what literature *means* is in part a spin-off from reader-centered criticism, with its reaction against the tendency of formalist criticism to treat works of literature as self-contained artistic objects. Since, however, some high-powered literary theorists continue to argue that literature makes no truth claims,

A recent writer has shown that as readers of literature we inevitably operate on the assumption of a writer's "inferred intention" even in regard to the genre of a work.[110] When we have reason to believe that a story is historically factual, we interpret the work accordingly, that is, with an eye on the correspondences between the story and a set of facts in empirical history. If we understand a work to be fictional, we do not look for such correspondences but treat it as self-contained. If we conclude that a poem is a lyric, we read it looking for feeling and reflection, but not for narrative. If we know that a piece of writing is satire, we accept exaggerations as a normal part of the work, but if we encounter exaggerations in an autobiography we do not accept them as a statement of truth. The point is that virtually everything we do as readers, even in matters of literary form, is based on the assumption of an intended meaning in the work.

Levels of Truth in Literature

Chapter 4 has already discussed some ways by which to determine the themes that have been embodied in a story or poem. Recall, too, the levels at which literature can be "true." It can be true to human experience or to our sense of

the following sources might prove valuable. The most convenient starting point is an essay by Gerald Graff entitled "Literature as Assertions," in *American Criticism in the Poststructuralist Age,* ed. Ira Konigsberg (Ann Arbor: University of Michigan Press, 1981), pp. 135–61. In this essay, Graff concludes that there are two good reasons for "accepting the claim that literary works make assertions. Briefly put, the arguments are that authors intend assertions and readers can scarcely help looking for them." For a full-scale scholarly treatment, one can consult Graff's book *Literature Against Itself* (Chicago: University of Chicago Press, 1979). Also helpful: Sheldon Sacks, *Fiction and the Shape of Belief* (Berkeley: University of California Press, 1964), especially the last chapter; and Morris Weitz, *Philosophy in Literature* (Detroit: Wayne State University Press, 1963).

the way things are (the reality principle), as when a love poem accurately captures the emotions of being in love.

Literature can also be true at the level of what I call "general truth." By this I mean that the themes of literature can be stated in very broad terms. For example, the *Odyssey* by the Greek poet Homer shows us the importance of home and family. Wordsworth's poetry lets us know that nature is a source of beauty and has a healing effect on the human psyche. D. H. Lawrence's stories assert that sex is an inevitable part of human life.

Milton said that truth is like the body of Osiris, fragmented and scattered. When we find general themes in literature, we are finding pieces of the truth. Without belittling the value of these pieces of truth that we find when we formulate the themes of literature in very general terms, I would also insist that truth in literature exists at a much more profound and specific level than such "general truth."

Works of literature also imply statements about ultimate truth. They embody a world view and are comments about human values and morality. They are, moreover, assertions about what really exists.

What Is a World View?

This is a way of saying that we cannot get along in the study of literature without knowing what a world view is and how to find it in works of literature. Here, then, are four definitions of a world view. Sigmund Freud, the founder of psychoanalysis, defined it as

> an intellectual construction, which gives a unified solution to all the problems of our existence in virtue of a comprehensive hypothesis, a construction, therefore, in which no question is left open and in which everything in which we are interested finds a place. . . . When one believes in such a thing, one feels secure in life, one knows what one

ought to strive after, and how one ought to organize one's emotions and interests to the best purpose.[111]

In his book *How to Read Slowly*, evangelical editor and author James Sire defines a world view as "a map of reality. . . . All of us carry around such a map in our mental make-up, and we act on it. All of our thinking presupposes it. Most of our experience fits into it."[112] Alvin Toffler, author of *Future Shock* and *The Third Wave*, writes:

> Every person carries within his head a mental model of the world—a subjective representation of reality. This model consists of tens upon tens of thousands of images. . . . We may think of this mental model as a fantastic internal warehouse, an image emporium in which we store our inner portraits . . . , along with such sweeping propositions as "Man is basically good" or "God is dead."[113]

The definition I have found most helpful is the one that describes a world view as "the framework of beliefs, expressive symbols, and values in terms of which individuals define their world, express their feelings, and make their judgments."[114]

Each of these definitions is useful. The first two show a philosopher's bias to regard a world view as made up only of ideas, while the second pair does a better job of doing justice to the way in which images, symbols, and feelings are also important in a world view. In kernel form, these definitions assert that a world view is a coherent view of life made up of basic assumptions and an integrating central value. A world view is both an *ideology* (a set of ideas) and a *mythology* (a set of images, stories, symbols, and heroes). It also includes such nonverbal qualities as emotions and attitudes.*

---

*Anyone who doubts this last statement should consider the way in which "insiders" at a church service or political rally or rock concert resonate with what is said and done, while "outsiders" are either unmoved or repelled. The thing

Every person has a world view on the basis of which he or she lives and makes decisions. Major works of literature also exhibit a world view. How, then, does a reader go about determining the nature of the world view in a given work of literature? It is not a hard process. Good readers do it naturally. To make the process more precise and complete, I share the methods that I have found most useful.†

1. The Highest Value and Integrating Core

Works of literature elevate something to the status of highest value and relate the rest of life to it. The highest value might be God, a person (self, a specific individual, humanity in general), an abstract quality (love, truth, beauty, order, reason, emotion), or nature. In Homer's *Odyssey*, it is home and family. In the epic *Aeneid*, by the Roman poet Virgil, the state is the supreme value.

Finding the World View in a Literary Work

In Romantic poetry, it is nature. In much modern literature, it is the physical drives and appetites (C. S. Lewis calls it "liberation of impulses"). To read "world viewishly," then, means first of all noticing the central value around which a work is built—the "fundamental hypothesis about the nature of existence which . . . introduces structure and coherence . . . into the formless stuff of life."[115]

that differentiates the two groups is more than differing ideas; it is also a complex of feelings and attitudes that they either share or don't share toward what is happening at the event.

†The book on world view that has helped me the most is the following, written from a general perspective: Richard Stevens and Thomas J. Musial, *Reading, Discussing, and Writing About the Great Books* (Boston: Houghton Mifflin, 1970); this paperback book went out of print almost at once and may be hard to locate. Two standard treatments from a Christian perspective are Harry Blamires, *The Christian Mind* (London: S.P.C.K., 1966), and James Sire, *The Universe Next Door: A Basic World View Catalog* (Downers Grove: InterVarsity Press, 1976).

2. Basic Premises

In addition to such an integrating core, a world view in literature consists of basic premises about life. Every long work of literature, and every collection of short poems, is an implied comment about the three great issues of life:

1. *Reality.* What really exists? The observable world? A supernatural or spiritual world? Meaning and design in the world?
2. *Morality.* What constitutes good and bad behavior?
3. *Values.* What is of worth in human experience? What really matters? What matters most?

3. The "World" of a Story or Poem

Furthermore, works of literature have their own "world." Someone has described the situation thus:

> In a work of art, whether it be a work of literature, a painting, or a work of some other art form, there is presented to us a special world, with its own space and time, its own ideological system, and its own standards of behavior. In relation to that world, we assume (at least in our first perceptions of it) the position of an alien spectator, which is necessarily external. Gradually, we enter into it, becoming more familiar with its standards, accustoming ourselves to it, until we begin to perceive this world as if from within.[116]

The world of a story or poem is offered to the reader as a picture of reality. Part of identifying the world view of a work, therefore, consists of paying attention to what is included and omitted from the picture. The following questions are good ones to ask when getting "inside" the world of a piece of literature:

1. What do the writer and/or characters in the work value most? For what do they strive? What motivates them?
2. According to the writer and/or characters,

what really exists? The physical world? A supernatural world? If so, what is the nature of each? Do moral qualities such as good and evil and love and courage really exist? Do relationships among people or loyalties to institutions exist, or is only the individual regarded as real? What is true about human nature? Is a person physical? Emotional? Moral/spiritual?

3. According to the writer and/or characters, how should life be lived? What constitutes the good life? What constitutes moral behavior toward other people or toward the physical world? How, if at all, can people have a relationship with God?

4. According to the writer and/or characters, what *brings* human fulfillment or happiness? Virtue? Pleasure? Sex? Physical objects? Money? God?

The world of a story or poem is one good clue to the overall world view that it embodies. This is why the novelist Flannery O'Connor writes that "it is from the kind of world the writer creates, from the kind of character and detail he invests it with, that a reader can find the intellectual meaning of a book."[117] It is important to realize additionally that what is *excluded* from the world of a literary work tells as much as what is *included*.

4. A Story As an Experiment in Living

If the work you are analyzing is a story (and I include plays in this category), the following scheme also works well. Stories are built around a central character (the protagonist). One of the most basic rules of interpretation is to pay attention to what happens to the protagonist. We should, moreover, regard the protagonist as undertaking an experiment in living that he or she pursues to its logical conclusion. The way in which the experiment ends is an implied comment on its adequacy or inadequacy.

Reading stories in this way is based on the

assumption that what happens to the protagonist is in some sense universal and representative or symbolic of a bigger pattern. If this is what happened to a particular character who did this particular thing, we reason, it is an example of a principle that is built into the fabric of reality and as such applies more universally. Here is the statement that I have found especially helpful in this regard:

> Ideally, the reader will be drawn into a confrontation with the protagonist. . . . We should consider the hero as one who makes an ultimate experiment—as one taking some line of action which in effect tests the kind of life he believes in. This way of reading considers the character . . . as one who pursues his experiment to its final stages and within a situation of ultimate meaning. Meaning in fiction is thus viewed as what an action leads to, results in, or implies.[118]

This framework can easily be broken down into a series of questions that, along with the earlier ones I mentioned, will aid in finding the world view of a piece of literature:

1. What is the basic identity of the characters, especially the protagonist? What motivates the characters? What are their preoccupations, as revealed by their thoughts, words, and actions? What do they value most and work to obtain?
2. What kind of action do the characters (especially the protagonist) undertake? What is the precise nature of the experiment in living? What things test it or stand it its way?
3. What are the results that follow from persons living and acting as these characters did? Does the protagonist succeed or fail in the experiment in living?

The way in which the story ends is, of course, crucial in interpreting the world view. If the experiment succeeds, the work as a whole asserts the adequacy of the world view that the story has tested. If the experiment fails, the work as a whole has established its viewpoint by negative example. Usually such a work implies an alternate world view to the one that has been exposed as inadequate. Consider, for example, the novel *Great Expectations* by nineteenth-century England's Charles Dickens. In this work the hero fails in his attempt to find happiness in a life of wealth, but in addition to showing us the failure of that experiment, the story suggests alternatives (contentment with a simple life, selfless love, honest work, for example). Often, in such cases, minor characters in the story serve as foils (contrasts) to the main character's negative experience.

The experiment-in-living concept that I have been discussing works best for stories, including plays. It can usually be applied also to a whole collection of lyric poems. Individual lyric poems, however, tend to assert their world view more directly. They are too short to include an experiment in living that leads to a conclusion. With poems like this, the best approach to world view is the framework of the "world" that emerges from the poem and the implied attitude in the poem toward such issues as God, humanity, and nature. I would also caution that we should not try to get more intellectual mileage out of an individual lyric poem than it is designed to yield. A lyric poem cannot cover the whole territory of a given topic. It captures a moment, a mood, a feeling. We must not extend such a fragment into a whole world view unless the poem itself makes certain implied claims about ultimate issues.

A Caution About Not Reducing Literature to Abstract Ideas

There is a danger that we must be aware of when we look for world views in literature. It is the danger of reducing literature to a set of abstract ideas, as though this is what literature exists for. In the process, the story or poem itself becomes superfluous. Works of literature *embody* and *incarnate* a world view. In talking about that world view in the terms I have outlined, we inevitably formulate it in conceptual terms. But this conceptual framework should never become a substitute for the work itself. It should only be a light by which to illuminate the story or poem. Literature *images forth* a world view. It allows us to experience and feel that world view as experientially as possible. In effect, we look at the world through the "eyes" of the writer's world view. We can diagram it thus:

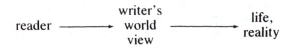

reader ⟶ writer's world view ⟶ life, reality

For this process to occur, a reader must enter as fully as possible into the entire imagined world of the story or poem. Even when we are analyzing literature for its world view, we must remember T. S. Eliot's great principle that literature should be approached as literature and "not defined in terms of something else."[119] Modern literary critic Sheldon Sacks expressed the same truth in different words: "The more precise our knowledge of how a writer has accomplished the artistic end of his work, the more accurate will be the inferences we make about his ethical beliefs, notions, prejudices."[120]

The Value of Encountering the World Views of Literature

Why is it important to encounter the world views that have been embodied in literature? It is a worthwhile form of knowledge for several reasons. It gives us a historical perspective on our own civilization and spares us the naïveté of beginning anew with each generation. Knowing the world views of literature also helps us to understand people who live by them today. An awareness of the important world views gives us a knowledge of the alternatives from which to choose our own world view. C. S. Lewis has written that "to judge between one *ethos* and another, it is necessary to have got inside both, and if literary history does not help us to do so it is a great waste of labour."[121]

The question of world view as I have discussed it thus far is of interest to any thoughtful person. Reading "world viewishly" is the best refutation of a common fallacy that reading literature does not engage a person's mind.

World View and the Christian Reader

If the world views of literature are important in this way for every reader, they also have some particular applications to Christian readers. All that I will say on the subject is contained in kernel form in this oft-quoted statement by T. S. Eliot:

> Literary criticism should be completed by criticism from a definite ethical and theological standpoint. . . . It is . . . necessary for Christian readers to scrutinize their reading, especially of works of imagination, with explicit ethical and theological standards. . . . What I believe to be incumbent upon all Christians is the duty of maintaining consciously certain standards and criteria of criticism over and above those applied by the rest of the world; and that by these criteria and standards everything that we read must be tested.[122]

Notice what all is implied by Eliot's statement. He envisions a two-stage process. The first, we should agree, is to see the work of literature as it really is in itself (to use Matthew Arnold's famous formula). This is largely a descriptive task, and it is one that any good reader or critic does. Christian literary criticism starts where every other kind of criticism starts—with the attempt to understand and enjoy the work as fully as possible on its own merits. Only *after* the work has been allowed to communicate its meanings should a Christian reader complete the task. I have heard and read far too much literary criticism from Christians who were entirely too quick to leap to a theological assessment, as though this is all that matters.

We should not exaggerate the distinctiveness of what Christian readers/critics do with literature. They take the descriptive process a step further than other critics do, or a step in a particular direction that may not interest others. But they are not engaging in any type of bizarre activity. Having described the work of literature as it really is in itself, Christian readers and critics usually go on to describe the relationship between the work and a Christian world view. This is not an esoteric activity, though it may be uninteresting to some non-Christians. Christian readers have their own agenda of interests, as do other readers.

Comparing Literature With a Christian World View

Eliot speaks of completing one's analysis of literature by applying "explicit ethical and theological standards" to the work. This is the process of "integration" that we hear so much about in some Christian circles. To *integrate* simply means to bring two things together, in this case literature and Christianity. There is no need to mysticize the process. It is something rigorously intellectual. It is a *comparative process* in which the world view of a piece of literature is set beside Christian doctrine and morality.

In this comparative process, a reader might profitably ask three questions:

1. Does the world view in the work of literature conform or fail to conform to Christian doctrine or ethics? (The answer may well be mixed for a given work.)
2. If some of the ideas and values are Christian, are they inclusively or exclusively

Christian? That is, are they ideas that *include* both Christianity and other religious or philosophic viewpoints, or do they *exclude* Christianity from other viewpoints? (We might visualize two circles, one representing Christianity and the other representing other religious viewpoints. The overlapping area of agreement constitutes inclusively Christian material; the part of the circle representing Christianity that does not overlap is exclusively Christian material. The ideas in most works of literature are inclusively Christian. In any case, the purpose of this scheme is to force a more careful scrutiny of what we read, not to encourage us to pigeonhole the ideas in works of literature.)

3. If some of the ideas and values in a work are Christian, are they a relatively complete version of the Christian view, or are they a relatively superficial or rudimentary version of Christian belief on a given topic?

An Outline of a
Christian World
View

Readers cannot answer these questions without first knowing what makes up a Christian world view. All the categories that I applied to world views in general have a specific Christian content as well.

For example, in a Christian, theistic world view, God is the center of reality and the one who gives identity to all other aspects of existence. In such a world view, people are defined as creatures of God. God also defines what the (human) self is, namely, the image of God. Moral goodness becomes defined as doing God's will. Time and history are identified as the working out of God's purpose. The state is viewed as a divinely ordained social institution established by God. Knowledge, in a Christian world view, is the truth that God reveals, and reality itself is regarded as God's creation. In short, a theistic world view is one in which God is the point of reference for all experience—the one who gives meaning and identity to every aspect of life. The specifically Christian world view places the triune God of the Bible at the center of reality and orders experience by the truth that God has revealed in the Bible and the incarnate life of Christ.

On the questions of reality, morality, and values, a Christian world view also has its specific beliefs. In a Christian world view, the unseen spiritual world (including heaven and hell) is as real as the visible sensory world. Since the subject of literature is human experience, the Christian view of human nature keeps coming up in literary criticism. Christianity postulates a threefold view of people: perfect and good in principle as created by God, fallen and therefore inclined to evil if left to themselves, and capable of being redeemed by God. The Bible is filled with moral commands and prohibitions, as well as moral examples in its stories, and these become crucial when conducting a critique of the moral viewpoints in literature.

Biblical Christianity is comprehensive. It has something to say on all of the issues raised by works of literature. One good general framework for an outline of a Christian world view is that provided by contemporary English author Harry Blamires in his book *The Christian Mind*. It lists the following as important areas in which the Christian mind has a distinctive outlook: its supernatural orientation, its awareness of evil, its conception of truth as God's revelation, its acceptance of God and the Bible as the ultimate authority, its concern for the person, its sacramental cast. To these we should add the central Christian doctrines of creation, fall, redemption, providence, and the consummation of history.

For Christian readers, one of the great *benefits* of conducting the type of comparative analysis I have been outlining is that it sends them constantly to the Bible and Christian theology and ethics to determine what Christianity teaches on the topics raised by works of literature. In the process, one's understanding of the Christian world view keeps getting expanded, better focused, and refined. Socrates said that the unexamined life is not worth living; Christians should be at least as thoughtful about their own world view.

The Bible As the Standard by Which Truth Is Measured

When T. S. Eliot speaks of testing what we read by "explicit ethical and theological standards," he obviously envisions a framework of belief that stands outside of the work of literature. That system of belief is the Christian world view. It is based ultimately on the Bible, though Christian creeds and writings by Christian thinkers can contribute to our understanding of a biblical world view. If someone wonders why I make the Bible the ultimate source of a Christian world view, the answer is simple: Christianity is a *revealed* religion. Its revelation is the Bible, the one common denominator among Christian denominations, even when creeds separate them.

The fact that a Christian reader is committed to a biblical standard of truth and morality has important implications for the question raised in the title of this chapter. *Does* literature tell the truth? At the level of world view, the answer is never an automatic "yes," though some enthusiasts for literature (including some Christian ones) sometimes give that impression. Each work of literature needs to be scrutinized on its own merits.

During the actual reading of a work of literature, we enter into the world of the work and vicariously look at the world through the writer's world view. But in the second, more reflective stage of analysis, we look at the work through the "lens" of our own world view. For a Christian reader, the situation can be diagrammed this way:

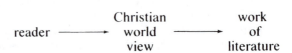

As Christian readers thus look at literature from the perspective of their own world view, the viewpoints in the work of literature either come into focus or remain blurred.

This is only a specific application of a principle that is practiced by every reader. *Every reader agrees or disagrees with the world view in works of literature on the basis of his or her own system of beliefs and values.* On the other hand, Christian readers are likely to have a stronger commitment to standards of truth that they regard as ultimate than many people in our relativistic age do. Christian readers have in their minds a New Testament statement about the need to "test the spirits to see if they are of God" (1 John 4:1). The process of comparison that I have outlined is a way of intellectually testing the spirits encountered in literature.

There Is More to Literature Than a World View

In thus applying rigorous standards of truth to literature, Christian readers need to respect the multiplicity of things that make up a work of literature. The truth or falseness of a work's world view is *one* aspect of it, but it is not the whole picture. There is usually much for Christian readers to relish and admire and affirm in works of literature whose world view has been weighed in the balance and found wanting. There is the level of form, skill, and craftsmanship. There is the criterion of faithfulness to human experience. And there are the broad themes that I have called "general truth."

In rejecting the world view of a work, we are not forced to condemn other aspects of it. I have sometimes been pained to see Christian readers act as though a work of literature has no value whatsoever because its world view is less than Christian. Of course, the reverse also happens: Christian readers who like other aspects of a work sometimes wrongly feel obliged to defend its world view as being Christian, even when it is not. A lot of mischief has been done by readers and critics who fail to distinguish the variety of facets in literature—even the multiple levels at which we can speak of its being "true."

When Christians look at the whole canon of literature through the lens of a Christian world view, they find that it falls into three big groupings. One is what I call *the literature of common humanity.* This is literature that in very general terms we would recognize as being true to life as we know it, with its anxieties, its longings, its enduring elements. A smaller category is *Christian literature*—literature that affirms the Christian world view.

Some Categories of Literature

There is, finally, the branch of literature that runs counter to Christian belief and perhaps is actively hostile to it. I call such literature *the literature of clarification* because it clarifies the non-Christian attitudes and world views by which people have always lived and continue to live. Such literature identifies the places where people seek for ultimate meaning when they do not find it in God: nature, love, sex, money, success, fame, human institutions. For a Christian, the value of reading such literature is high—*it clarifies the human situation to which the Chris 'an faith speaks!*

Readers who attempt to measure the truth or falseness of literature by the standard of the Christian world view have not always found it easy to avoid certain abuses. One such abuse is unduly *minimizing* the Christian element in

Some Abuses to Avoid

literature—not seeing Christianity where it exists in works of literature. A subspecies of this abuse is too hastily leaping to a negative theological assessment without showing any sensitivity to the artistry or partial truthfulness of a work, or even to its integrity as a work of literature. The opposite abuse is even more prevalent and consists of *seeing Christianity where it doesn't exist*. Some critics stretch the terms "religious" and "Christian" so far that virtually all of literature is included in those categories. A related abuse is *allegorizing* works of literature to make them (supposedly) embody Christian doctrine or the life of Christ, or collecting *analogues* (parallels) between details in a work of literature and something in the Bible.

Some critics who purport to examine literature from a Christian perspective have engaged in methods that are alarming to the orthodox believer. Particularly noteworthy is that huge branch of criticism (the product of a secular age) that *equates* literature and Christianity, in effect making literature and the imagination a substitute for the Christian faith. It is possible, also, to find critics making judgments about the Christian element in works of literature based on an inaccurate definition of Christianity.*

SUMMARY

Stories and poems embody a world view—a picture of reality, morality, and values. They are built around a central integrating value that defines every aspect of life.

Christian readers are committed to a Christian world view. Consequently, one thing that they do with a work of literature is compare its world view with their own. In this comparative process, their awareness of their own world view is sharpened, expanded, and exercised.

Christians cannot afford the narrow vision

*I say more about some of these abuses in *Triumphs of the Imagination: Literature in Christian Perspective* (Downers Grove: InterVarsity Press, 1979), pp. 233–39.

that comes from reading only works that es-
pouse a Christian world view. They need to
assimilate the impact of other world views as a
way of learning to understand and respect
people who live by such world views even
though they disagree with those people and
world views.

The intellectual usefulness of literature is not
that it always tells the truth, which it may or
may not do. Instead, by embodying world views,
literature acts as a catalyst to our thinking, both
about our own world view and the diversity of
viewpoints that we encounter in our culture.

chapter seven

Literature
and Morality

Literature is preoccupied with human behavior. It is therefore inevitably concerned with moral issues. The subject of literature and morality is complex and controversial. The morality of literature involves the subject matter of literary works, the moral perspective of such works, and the effect of literature on the behavior of readers.

It has been almost a century since Oscar Wilde, the outrageous British author and critic, wrote, "There is no such thing as a moral or an immoral book. Books are well written, or badly written. That is all."[123] Those famous words signaled the end of one era and the beginning of another.

Prior to the end of the last century, few of the great literary critics questioned that literature

Does Literature Have Moral Implications?

153

has moral implications. Virtually all of them contribute something to the ongoing discussion about what makes literature moral or immoral.*

To Plato we owe insights into the affective nature of literature (its ability to move a reader), into the emotional appeals that literature makes to a reader (appeals that Plato, with his classical bias against the emotions, distrusted), and into the influence produced on readers by fictional models of behavior.[124] Aristotle gives us the provocative comment that moral literature "satisfies the moral sense."[125] We can thank Sir Philip Sidney for a zestful endorsement of the potential moral good that flows from the ability of literature to move a reader; according to Sidney, this potential for good resides especially in the moral examples of behavior embodied in literature.[126] Wordsworth and the Romantics declared that the emotional power of literature is not, as Plato thought, inherently immoral but can be moral; in Wordsworth's great phrase, moral literature leaves a reader's "affections strengthened and purified."[127] And the Victorian critic Matthew Arnold theorized that if literature deals with human experience—with the question of "how to live"—it cannot avoid issues of morality, "because human life itself is in so preponderating a degree moral."[128]

At the end of the last century, various forces converged to make it unfashionable to discuss the moral dimension of literature. That moral vacuum in literary criticism continued for nearly a century. There were some low moments in that interval. No less a literary giant than Ernest Hemingway wrote, "What is moral is what you feel good after and what is immoral is what you feel bad after."[129]

More recently, the topic of morality and

---

*For an overview of the history of moral criticism of literature, the best starting point is Keith F. McKean, *The Moral Measure of Literature* (Westport, Conn.: Greenwood Press, 1961). One should also go directly to the primary texts that I cite in the next paragraph.

literature has suddenly become fashionable—
and controversial. In 1978, novelist John Gardner published a book entitled *On Moral Fiction*
(New York: Basic Books). It is not what I
consider a good treatment of the topic, but the
effect of the book was striking. Two years after
its appearance, Gardner's book elicited an
anthology of fiction by various authors entitled
An Anthology of Moral Fiction (ed. Joe David
Bellamy). More important than the fiction in the
volume is an introductory forum in which
twenty-eight authors responded to Gardner's
book, in an overwhelmingly hostile manner.

Despite the hostility of writers to the call for
moral literature, the relationship between literature and morality is an increasing preoccupation
among critics. Statements such as the following
suggest the current climate of criticism:

> The teaching of literature inevitably involves the
> conscious or unconscious reinforcement of ethical
> attitudes. It is practically impossible to treat any
> novel or drama, or indeed any literary work of art,
> in a vital manner without confronting some problem
> of ethics and without speaking out of the context of
> some social philosophy. . . . The teacher would do
> neither literature nor students a service if he tried to
> evade ethical issues.[130]

> No work of literature is a "purely" aesthetic
> experience, divorced from any moral consider-
> ation. . . . It does not state its values but acts them
> out in such a way that they are judged through the
> very manner of enactment.[131]

> Moral standards . . . are as relevant to literature as
> they are to life itself. . . . If the subject matter of
> literary art is the full range of human values, then
> ethical principles are always relevant. . . . If litera-
> ture itself is an evaluation of experience, both
> explicitly and by implication, then any adequate
> judgment of the art must measure the evaluation by
> the critic's own moral standards.[132]

It is not hard to find critics who claim that
the morality of literature is a necessary part of a
reader's concern. To date, however, such

discussions have remained at such a vague level of generality that the critic's actual moral standards remain evasive.* We are the heirs of a permissive culture, and for a critic actually to come out and assert that a given book is immoral is extremely rare.

The secular element in our culture sometimes tries to foist on us the impression that concern over the immoral effects of literature is an aberration of a fanatic religious fringe of society. This is untrue. Great writers themselves have been shocked by the immorality of some literature. In a famous passage, William Wordsworth writes about the literature of his day,

> For a multitude of causes, unknown to former times, are now acting with a combined force to blunt the discriminating powers of the mind, and, unfitting it for all voluntary exertion, to reduce it to a state of almost savage torpor. . . . To this tendency of life and manners the literature and theatrical exhibitions of the country have conformed themselves. . . . When I think upon this degrading thirst after outrageous stimulation, I am almost ashamed to have spoken of the feeble endeavour made in these volumes to counteract it.[133]

In a similar vein, Samuel Taylor Coleridge wrote, "The longer I live, the more I am impressed with the exceeding immorality of

---

*Most of the recent interest in the morality of literature has ignored Christian dimensions, and I have not found the discussions very helpful. Some of the main sources, in addition to Gardner's book, are these: Wayne C. Booth, *The Rhetoric of Fiction* (Chicago: University of Chicago Press, 1961, 1983), chap. 13; Graham Hough, *The Dream and the Task: Literature and Morals in the Culture of Today* (London: Gerald Duckworth, 1963); Sheldon Sacks, *Fiction and the Shape of Belief* (Berkeley: University of California Press, 1964); R. W. Beardsmore, *Art and Morality* (London: Macmillan, 1971). Discussions from a Christian perspective include Harold C. Gardiner, *Norms for the Novel*, rev. ed. (Garden City: Hanover House, 1960); Edmund Fuller, *Man in Modern Fiction* (New York: Random House, 1949); Leland Ryken, *Triumphs of the Imagination: Literature in Christian Perspective* (Downers Grove: InterVarsity Press, 1979), pp. 175–90.

modern plays: I can scarcely refrain from anger. . . ."[134] T. S. Eliot is even blunter: "Contemporary literature as a whole tends to be degrading."[135]

The issue of morality and literature has historically been regarded as significant, and it is so regarded today. It is a complex issue, as the following discussion will suggest.

As a foundation for exploring the relationship between morality and literature, we need to define some terms. Let me say at once that this chapter is not about censorship. It is an index to the paranoia that exists in some circles today that the word "censorship" immediately arises when the topic of morality and literature is mentioned. I am concerned at a theoretic level with the relationship between morality and literature. My remarks have a lot to say about how individual readers can insure the morality of their own reading experiences, but I am definitely not talking about the procedural question of how to curb the immoral tendencies of literature in society at large.

Defining Some Issues

In the previous chapter I discussed the issue of the truthfulness of literature. The morality of literature should not be confused with its intellectual truth or falseness, though the two have some overlapping concerns. Morality has to do with human behavior, especially between one person and another. The morality of literature, therefore, will focus primarily on the models of behavior in works of literature, not on their implied philosophic assertions.

This means that not every work whose world view is untruthful will appear to be immoral. Most literature I teach fails to affirm a Christian world view and scale of values, yet I would not hesitate to claim that most of this literature is moral. We can also predict that the morality of literature will be a much bigger issue with stories and plays (which focus on characters in action) than with lyric poems (though these can also recommend certain patterns of behavior for a reader's approval).

It is often assumed that when critics are concerned about the moral dimension of literature they ignore the artistic side of literature. This is not necessarily the case. Any moral effect that a work produces stems from something *in* the work itself. Literature gains its moral impact through literary *form*—through characters and events and the sentiments embodied in lyric poems. Twentieth-century literary critic Elder Olson describes the fusion of artistic and ethical aspects of literature in this way:

> It is not that art teaches by precept, as older generations thought, nor that it moves to action; but clearly it inculcates moral attitudes; it determines our feelings toward characters of a certain kind for no other reason than that they are such characters. The ethical function of art, therefore, is never in opposition to the purely artistic end; on the contrary, it is best achieved when the artistic end has been best accomplished, for it is only a further consequence of the powers of art.[136]

In discussing the moral aspect of literature we are not abandoning its literary dimension but, if anything, are scrutinizing it more closely.

Given the four ingredients in any literary situation—world, author, work, audience—the question of morality concerns primarily two of them—the moral tendencies embodied *in* the work and the effect of those tendencies *on* the audience.

The logical starting point is the work itself. No matter how crucial the reader's response is in determining the morality or immorality of a work of literature, it is obvious that a reader's response is always a response *to* a stimulus, the work itself. What, then, should we scrutinize about a story or poem when assessing its morality?

We can begin with the models of behavior that a writer selects for portrayal. Simply by portraying certain types of behavior, a writer is capable of creating a moral or immoral response in a reader. Literary theorists have recognized this as far back as Plato, who was troubled by the effect produced by the literary portrayal of immoral behavior:

159
Literature
and Morality

The Moral
Dimension of
Literary Subject
Matter

> Now can we be right in praising and admiring another who is doing that which any one of us would abominate and be ashamed of in his own person? . . . Few persons ever reflect . . . that the contagion must pass from others to themselves.[137]

The principle underlying Plato's statement is an important one, namely, that literature is a stimulus to a response, a stimulus that works partly by presenting images of human behavior which a reader is capable of imitating.

Plato is wrong in claiming that the portrayal of immoral conduct "must" (his word) automatically lead a reader to emulate it, but that it can do so is indisputable. The Christian novelist Francois Mauriac once received a photograph from a reader of one of his books with an accompanying note that stated, "To the man who nearly made me kill my grandmother."[138]

Closer to home, *Newsweek* carried an article describing how three youths murdered a professor in a manner similar to that portrayed in a recent horror movie.[139] An article in *Reader's Digest* entitled "TV Violence: The Shocking New Evidence" multiplied similar examples.[140] Almost simultaneously with those articles there appeared in *The American Scholar* an article that speculated on the meaning of the fact that musician John Lennon's assassin was carrying a copy of *Catcher in the Rye* when he committed the murder, and that he read a passage from the novel at his trial.[141] These examples show what *can* happen, not what *must* happen.

Before we jump to the conclusion that literature that portrays immoral behavior is necessarily immoral, we should pause to note that literature can embody a moral viewpoint by negative example, that is, by exposing the evil of the immoral behavior that is presented. Moral literature not only presents exemplary characters but also realistically portrays evil and depravity. The Bible itself portrays an abundance of immoral behavior—violence, cruelty, adultery, rape, homosexuality, murder, lying, stealing, and a dozen others. Yet we would not consider the Bible an immoral book.

Then, too, literature is a great repository of positive models of moral behavior, and not simply of *im*moral behavior. We tend to hear too much about the negative models in literature and not enough about the positive models. As Sir Philip Sidney observed with enthusiasm in *An Apology for Poetry,* literature has an unparalleled ability to move readers to virtuous behavior when it supplies them with models of moral virtue.

**How the Subject
Matter of
Literature
Influences a
Reader**

At the ground level of subject matter, then, literature can be either moral or immoral as an influence. The literature that we read and view is one of the chief sources of the images (including models of behavior and representative characters) with which we fill our minds and imaginations. These images become the habitual furniture of our minds. Some images are refining and redemptive and sanctifying in their moral influence. To quote Sidney, some literature encourages the will "to that which deserveth to be called and accounted good."[142] Other images are coarse, cheapening, and degrading in their impact. In the words of Sidney, there are types of literature that "infect the fancy [imagination] with unworthy objects."[143] I have often been struck by the phrase that Geoffrey Chaucer, the greatest of the medieval English poets, used in his "Retraction," where he asks Christ to forgive him for the stories in *The Canterbury Tales* "that tend toward sin." What did Chaucer have in mind? My guess is that he was thinking about the subject matter of his scatological and sexual scenes.

In the long run, we become the sum of our indulgences, including the books we read and the movies we watch. If we habitually fill our minds with images of sex, we begin to view people as sexual objects. Someone has estimated that by the time of high school graduation, the average American young person has vicariously participated in twenty thousand murders while watching fifteen thousand hours of television. What is the most common result? A dulling of reverence for life and a blunting of respect for the worth of people.

The strategy of literature is to give form to our own feelings and impulses. These inner impulses are a mixture of good and bad, waiting to be encouraged or discouraged by outward stimuli. The effect of some subject matter is to awaken the wrong impulses—impulses toward hatred or violence or sexual license or dishonesty or expediency or materialism. And the influence of other types of subject matter is to encourage good impulses—toward honesty or courage or self-control or compassion, for example. Even subject matter, therefore, can become a moral issue.

A further aspect is the cumulative effect that certain subject matter has on readers. An isolated instance can easily appear too trivial to make an issue over. Multiplied several dozen times, that same subject matter definitely becomes a moral influence. Alexander Pope, the major poet of the English Neo-Classical period, said something profound when he wrote,

Vice is a monster of so frightful mien,
As, to be hated, needs but to be seen;
Yet seen too oft, familiar with her face,
We first endure, then pity, then embrace.[144]

The subject matter of literature, then, is one aspect of its moral tendency. It would be easy to exaggerate its impact by itself. Literature that depicts immoral behavior, as the Bible certainly does, is not necessarily immoral literature. We should make a distinction between the subject matter of literature—its settings, characters, and events—and its theme or perspective. The effect of morally objectionable subject matter has to be judged in terms of the moral impact of the work as a whole. Some people have been too quick to judge as immoral a work that in isolated details portrays immorality but that in its overall viewpoint takes a moral attitude toward the evil thus portrayed.* Sheldon Sacks comments correctly that "a good novelist embodies his beliefs and opinions in such a way that a particularized ethical effect is an assured consequence of his *whole* novel."[145]

The Importance of the Moral Perspective in a Work

The moral *perspective* that writers build into their works is generally a more reliable guide to its morality or immorality than is subject matter considered by itself. When writers portray models of behavior, they ordinarily suggest an attitude toward that behavior. Even authorial silence about an event—a straightforward account of stealing or adultery, for example—can constitute a perspective. Stories or poems that treat adultery or selfishness or materialism as normal and acceptable are immoral in their viewpoint.

Literature is a calculated strategy to get a reader to approve of some things and disapprove of others. The attitude that writers embody within a work itself has a powerful influence on the reader's approval pattern. T. S. Eliot states the matter very concisely:

*For more on the need to read works as *wholes*, see Harold C. Gardiner, *Norms for the Novel;* and Irving and Cornelia Sussman, *How to Read a Dirty Book* (Chicago: Franciscan Herald Press, 1966).

When we read of human beings behaving in certain ways, with the approval of the author, who gives his benediction to this behavior by his attitude toward the result of the behavior arranged by himself, we can be influenced towards behaving in the same way.[146]

Notice how many ways writers can influence the moral response of a reader: through the models of behavior they put before a reader, through arranging the outcome of the behavior, through suggesting an attitude toward that outcome.

Sheldon Sacks analyzed how storytellers embodied their ethical viewpoints in the actual form or technique of a story and concluded that the final effect of a story

> depended heavily on how successful its creator was in controlling our sympathy and antipathy toward, our approval and disapproval of, characters, thoughts, and actions at every stage of his work. Such attempts to control are implicit in devices of disclosure. . . . A novelist selects both what he represents and how he represents it.[147]

Based on the idea that literature embodies a moral perspective within a work itself, we can define immoral literature as "literature which recommends immoral behaviour."[148] Literature has many ways of offering an immoral viewpoint for our approval: making immoral acts attractive; leaving goodness "bereft of its proper beauty";[149] generating ultimate sympathy for immoral characters; denigrating characters whose actions and attitudes are moral; taking the reader or viewer through a crime from the criminal's perspective rather than the victim's in such a way as to portray the crime as something that brings gratification; omitting moral characters and behavior that might serve as foils to the immoral ones and thereby offer the audience an alternative; treating immoral acts with a comic tone that prompts a reader to acquiesce, even if temporarily, in something immoral; portraying immoral acts as something that people have no choice in resisting; recommending moral acts (such as honesty or courage) only because they are expedient, not because they are morally right.

Moral literature, by contrast, is literature that "recommends moral as opposed to immoral behaviour."[150] The means by which a story or poem can incarnate such a moral bias include these: making the good appear attractive or ultimately satisfying (even though there may be a price tag for doing the right thing); showing that immoral acts do not bring ultimate satisfaction; displaying models of moral behavior in such a way as to make the reader wish to imitate them; generating final sympathy for moral characters; showing that crime always victimizes someone and is therefore not a positive thing; exposing the self-destructive nature of evil; including foils to immoral behavior as a way of showing that people have a power of choice to resist evil; unmasking the socially destructive consequences of evil.

Moral literature does not avoid evil as a subject, but it finds ways to discredit it. Calvin Seerveld, a contemporary scholar and author of numerous works on aesthetics, writes, "Art is Biblically Christian when the Devil cannot stand it. . . . The Devil cannot stand exposure of sin as sin, dirty, devastating misery for men; it unmasks him."[151] There is, in other words, a *moral* attitude that can be taken toward immorality. Harry Blamires writes in this regard, "There is nothing in our experience, however trivial, worldly, or even evil, which cannot be thought about christianly."[152]

The moral perspective that writers build into their works is usually not hard to sense. In the area of sexual morality, for example, we are in an immensely different world in the plays of Shakespeare, where the idealized lovers defer sexual consummation of their love until after marriage, than we are in the world of much modern literature, where promiscuous sex is portrayed as though it were a normal part of life. Someone has said that there are no "innocent" adulterers in Shakespeare; by contrast, most modern literature tries to convince us that promiscuous sex is normal and healthy.

To sum up: writers embody perspectives in their works both by virtue of the models of behavior that they choose to include in their works and the attitude they imply toward that behavior. My line of argument regarding what makes a work moral or immoral is capsulized in a comment that Coleridge made about the moral tone of Shakespeare:

Summary: Works of Literature Embody Moral Tendencies

> Shakespeare always makes vice odious and virtue admirable, while Beaumont and Fletcher do the very reverse—they ridicule virtue and encourage vice: they pander to the lowest and basest passions of our nature.[153]

Thus far I have discussed the moral tendencies inherent in a work of literature. This is the only aspect of the topic that many people think about, but in fact it is less decisive than the reader's actual response to what he or she reads.

The Heart of the Matter: The Reader's Response

If you doubt this, pause to consider the wide range of influences that the same work produces on different readers or viewers. How can we account for such variability of influence and response?

The mere words on a page are neither moral nor immoral in themselves. They are a potential stimulus, but a reader's response ultimately determines the precise nature of the effect that the stimulus creates. Books have never committed murder or adultery, have never stolen or lied. Nor have they performed moral feats of honesty or compassion or kindness. Literature becomes moral or immoral only as, and to the extent that, it is assimilated by a reader and translated into mental or behavioral acts.

No effect of literature is automatic, a fact that we too often forget. Even reading the Bible does not automatically produce moral behavior in readers. Throughout history people have used the Bible to defend such immoral acts as exploitation, racism, adultery, and assorted others. The same work of literature frequently has a moral influence on some readers and an immoral effect on others. The behavior of Mersault in French novelist Albert Camus's novel *The Stranger* elicits my repulsion, but from the day of its publication many readers have admired this protagonist as someone worthy of emulation. (Among other reprehensible acts, Mersault committed murder in the story and showed no remorse for his action.)

If the moral influence of literature is this subjective, we should be cautious about labeling a work as moral or stigmatizing it as immoral. It may be such for a given reader, but usually not for every reader. Who would call the Bible an immoral book because immoral people have used it perversely? The moral effect of literature on a given reader may even be based on a misreading of a work. Aldous Huxley's *Brave New World* strongly denounces the promiscuity that exists in the futuristic society portrayed in the book and even includes positive foils to the immorality; yet one reader recalls that throughout his adolescence the novel was for him a source of pornography.[154] Unless I know that a book is influencing a person in an immoral direction, I am inclined to refrain from passing judgment on others, even when I have censored the book for myself.

Contemporary literary theory defines literature as something that happens in a reader, not as words on a page. Whatever we may think of this theory in general, it points in the right direction when we consider the particular question of morality in literature.

Readers whose moral sense is healthy are very rarely swept into immorality when they encounter literature that recommends immoral behavior for their approval. The medieval storyteller Boccaccio wrote in this regard that "poets are not corruptors of morals. Rather, if the reader is prompted by a healthy mind, not a diseased one, they will prove actual stimulators to virtue."[155] Notice the key clause: "if the reader is prompted by a healthy mind, not a diseased one."

If moral readers can assimilate a work of literature in a positive way, contrary to a writer's intention, the reverse is also possible. Immoral readers can twist a work's inherent moral tendencies, or seize upon the portrayal of scenes depicting immoral behavior, in a perverse manner. Consider, for example, the following anonymous description of the Bible that I ran across: "This book is rated X. There is enough smut, enough downright rottenness to make this a bestseller almost everywhere. The book goes on for more than a thousand pages of vice, filth, corruption, and utter foulness, whatever goes into a bestseller these days. The authors can't wait to get the characters into the bedroom. The Bible is adult entertainment."

We can accurately speak of books having tendencies toward morality or immorality, as I did earlier in this chapter. But in the final analysis we are on safer ground if we think in terms of reading experiences, or even readers, as being moral or immoral. Is "My Last Duchess" by Victorian poet Robert Browning a moral or immoral poem? The question cannot be resolved by looking only at the text in isolation from a reader's response. For a professor who tries to convince a class that the duke is an immoral character, the poem is moral. For the class that claims to admire the duke, the poem has confirmed an immoral attitude.

How does this apply to Christian readers? For one thing, the time has come for Christians to stop being intimidated from talking about the morality of literature. Books and movies always stimulate a response. That response can be either good or bad, moral or immoral. Reading literature is not a neutral activity like riding in a car. It is much more like food that we digest by taking it into ourselves. What we read and view can either nurture or contaminate us morally.

Christian readers differ from most people in our culture by their concern about the moral impact of literature on themselves and their culture. Most people go to the latest movie or read the current bestseller without bothering to think about the morality of the experience. Plato said something profound about the moral effect of literature in a society when he wrote, "Great is the issue at stake, greater than appears: whether a person is to be good or bad."[156] Christians stand with Plato (and most of the other major literary theorists throughout history) and against modern trends on this matter.

**The Need for
Self-Awareness**

Christians can best begin by scrutinizing their own moral responses to the literature they read. Just as all education is ultimately self-education, the only effective type of censorship is self-censorship. Christian readers need to be aware of how what they read affects them morally.

If the effect is one that pushes a reader toward immoral attitudes, feelings, or behavior, the antidote is simple: either *stop reading* the troublesome material, or *exercise stronger moral control* over the influence the material is exerting. Works of literature are moral and immoral persuaders, but no reader is obliged to be persuaded against his or her will.

Because so much of the moral impact of literature depends on the reader, Christians can probably afford to be a little more relaxed about the moral impact of their own reading than they often are. What happens when readers who are committed to Christian standards of morality encounter literature that offers immoral behavior for their approval? They are usually repelled by the immorality that is commended and have their own moral resolve strengthened.

This desired effect will happen if Christian readers are aware of their moral responses to literature. Moral reading (as opposed to immoral reading) begins with awareness—awareness of how our reading is affecting our behavior and awareness of what a given work of literature is trying to move us to accept. We need to keep our guard up when we read literature. It is my observation that most Christians do, in fact, have their guards up in regard to literature, more than they do with advertising and television programs and popular music. Still, we must heed T. S. Eliot's warning that

> the author of a work of imagination is trying to affect us wholly, as human beings, . . . and we are affected by it, as human beings, whether we intend to be or not. . . . What we read does not concern merely something called our *literary taste*, but . . . affects directly, though only amongst other influences, the whole of what we are. . . . I incline to come to the alarming conclusion that it is just the literature that we read for "amusement," or "purely for pleasure" that may have the greatest and least suspected influence upon us.[157]

Christians Have Their Own Standards of Morality

I have been using the terms "moral" and "immoral" throughout this chapter as though they have an agreed meaning, but of course they do not. What people regard as moral or immoral depends on their standards of morality. It is at this point that Christians have no choice but to part company with the world at large, at least much of the time.

For a Christian, what is moral is what the Bible reveals to be moral. No book in the world says more about morality than the Bible does.

Its moral norms are stated in precepts and embodied in story and character. The Bible, moreover, is a remarkably comprehensive treatment of moral issues.

The moral standards that our culture at large applies to literature (including television and movies) are notoriously low and have been getting more permissive with each decade of our century. Biblical morality is far more rigorous than the morality of a secular society. For one thing, public morality is concerned with external behavior only, which partly accounts for the difficulty that our society has in dealing with pornography. Then, too, society at large tends to equate what is moral with what is legal. The sentiment that "you can't go to jail for what you're thinking," with the implication that anything for which you cannot be sent to jail is moral, expresses the ethic by which most people in our society live.

Biblical morality, by contrast, calls people to live by a far stricter standard than what is merely legal and what can be observed externally. Jesus' comments about the law (Matt. 5) are a classic passage on the subject, but the emphasis is everywhere present in the Bible. Most crucially, biblical morality includes the ideal of holiness and extends it to include thoughts, attitudes, and emotions, as well as overt actions.

The Need for Enlightened Literary Principles

Christian readers should have rigorous standards of morality in their reading of literature. But they must also be clear-sighted about what makes literature moral and immoral. They must know how works of literature embody moral tendencies. Then they must apply the principles accurately. Christians who have had the best intentions in regard to morality in literature have made charges against works of literature that they have simply misread. In the process, they have jeopardized the possibility of getting a fair hearing in the world at large. Frequently, for example, people have tried to eliminate from high school English courses such works as *Huckleberry Finn* and "The Lottery," a short story by modern writer Shirley Jackson. Though I understand the concerns of the protestors, and share their moral standards, these are not the works that need to be removed from the school curriculum.

Christians need to make a distinction between having their sensibilities offended and having undergone an immoral experience. I have encountered a lot of literary subject matter that offends standards of good taste or decency. I do not enjoy such literature and usually try to avoid it. But having my sensitivities shocked or irritated is quite different from having engaged in an immoral activity. Coleridge noted in this regard that "it is necessary to make a distinction between manners and morals"; in applying this principle to Shakespeare, Coleridge concluded that "in Shakespeare there are a few gross speeches, but it is doubtful to me if they would produce any ill effect on an unsullied mind."[158] A lot of Christian charges of immorality in literature have been cases of offensive material rather than an immoral perspective in a work as a whole.

Not only do Christians need to avoid inadequate judgments about what constitutes immoral literature; they also need enlightened standards for defining what makes literature *moral*. Moral literature is too often equated with literature that *moralizes*. The latter makes its moral point too obviously, too abstractly, without embodying its moral patterns in story or image, without earning the right to make its moral affirmations by looking at life steadily and whole, or by not trusting literature to achieve its effects by literary means. I am even inclined to think that literature is usually not strongly moral in its impact if it is not good literature in the first place. Literature has the power to move only when a writer respects the craft of literature, and that means avoiding abstractness and preachiness in deference to an incarnation of meaning in story and poetry. Good literature is not propaganda. I repeat part of the statement by Elder Olson that I quoted earlier in this chapter: "The ethical function of art . . . is best achieved when the artistic end has been best accomplished, for it is only a further consequence of the powers of art."

The idea of moral literature should be a liberating thing, not a constraining one. I associate it with the literature that I love most—with Homer and Shakespeare and Milton and Wordsworth and Tennyson and Browning and Dickens and T. S. Eliot. The criterion of moral literature, in fact, helps me to define one of the excellencies of these writers. The fact that reading these authors strengthens my moral life instead of assaulting it explains part of the delight I find in reading them. And on the other hand, having to fight against the moral tendencies of the other type of literature always detracts something from my reading of it, no matter how much I may enjoy other aspects of it.

I have on occasion been asked if some literature is not simply amoral, that is, between the definite categories of moral and immoral. I think so. I would even be charitably inclined to put such literature in the category of moral literature on the ground that most of this literature does, in subtle ways, produce a climate that is favorable to positive moral behavior.

Moral judgments are a necessary part of reading literature. But they are not *all* that Christian readers should look at in a work of literature. As readers, we also need to be open to the artistic and experiential aspects of literature. C. S. Lewis* has said that the Christian

---

*I quote Lewis's statement to suggest the *spirit* in which we should read literature, not to suggest that "comedies that merely amuse" are off-bounds to moral scrutiny. Comedy is in fact one of the strongest moral persuaders in our experience, often, I fear, in an immoral direction.

"has no objection to comedies that merely amuse and tales that merely refresh."[159] Thus, not every reading experience needs to be a solemnly moral exercise. There is no need to place demands on literature that we do not put on attending a ball game or going on a picnic. In our moments of recreation as elsewhere, however, we need to be aware of the moral impact of what we experience.

SUMMARY

For a Christian, all of life has moral implications. The reading of literature is no exception. Oscar Wilde's statement that "there is no such thing as a moral or an immoral book" falsifies both the nature of literature and what happens when we read.

Good literature deals powerfully with human conduct and thus always has moral implications. And because literature is a stimulus to a response, it necessarily has the potential to influence readers in either a moral or immoral direction.

The ultimate responsibility for the moral influence of literature rests with its readers.

chapter eight

Afterword

Literature serves many important functions in the lives of people and civilizations. Because its subject is human experience, literature heightens human awareness of reality. Literature is one of the means by which people grapple with and assimilate reality.

Literature also gives form to our feelings, experiences, and beliefs. As a human race we turn our joys into literature to prolong them and our sorrows into literature so we can bear them. Literature allows us to celebrate life and the experiences that are closest to us. It deepens our zest for life by giving us the words and images for expressing our affirmations and insights. It intensifies our involvement with life.

Furthermore, literature enlarges our being by admitting us to experiences and viewpoints other than our own. By expanding our range of   175 experiences, literature alerts us to the needs and problems of people around us. Literature enriches our sympathies.

Literature enhances our understanding of essential human nature. It is the most reliable repository of the hopes, longings, fears, and values of the human race. The archetypes (recurring images, plot motifs, and character types) of literature put us in touch with what is basic and enduring in human experience. The news tells us what happened; literature tells us what happens.

Literature interprets as well as presents human experience. This, too, enables it to heighten a reader's awareness of life. Literature is always an implied comment about what is good and bad, desirable and undesirable, moral and immoral. In reading literature, therefore, we encounter ideas and attitudes and a variety of world views. Some of these are cordial to us, others distasteful. In either case, literature is a catalyst to a person's thinking about the great issues of life. Literature helps us learn to ask the right questions about life. It allows for an exercise and sharpening of any reader's world view.

Literature is delightful as well as useful. It is a form of recreation and enjoyment, a potentially constructive form of leisure activity. By awakening our imaginations, literature emancipates us from our own time and place. Literature is an art form and as such a source of beauty in a person's life. It is also a glorious manifestation of human creativity.

Literature is a form of discovery, perception, intensification, expression, interpretation, creativity, beauty, and understanding. These are ennobling activities and qualities. For a Christian, they can be God-glorifying, a gift from God to the human race to be accepted with zest.

References

[1] Douglas C. Kimmel, *Adulthood and Aging: An Interdisciplinary, Developmental View* (New York: Wiley, 1973), pp. 434–35.

[2] R. F. Daubenmire, *Plants and Environment* (New York: Wiley, 1974), pp. 324–44.

[3] Mark Twain, *Life on the Mississippi,* chap. 30.

[4] Excerpt from Matthew Arnold's *Essays in Criticism, First Series,* as reprinted in *The Norton Anthology of English Literature,* 4th ed., ed. M. H. Abrams (New York: W. W. Norton, 1979), 2:1423.

[5] Louise M. Rosenblatt, *Literature as Exploration,* 3d ed. (New York: Noble and Noble, 1976), p. 38.

[6] Nathan A. Scott, Jr., *Modern Literature and the Religious Frontier* (New York: Harper and Brothers, 1958), p. 52.

[7] Joseph Conrad, *The Nigger of the Narcissus* (New York: Collier Books, 1962), preface, p. 19.

[8] C. S. Lewis, *An Experiment in Criticism* (Cambridge: Cambridge University Press, 1961), pp. 137–40.

[9] Ralph Waldo Emerson, "The Poet," in *Major Writers of America,* ed. Perry Miller (New York: Harcourt, Brace and World, 1962), 1:530–31.

[10] Samuel T. Coleridge, *Biographia Literaria,* chap. 4.

[11] The Gallup poll is cited by Arthur Schlesinger, Jr., "Implications of Leisure for Government," in *Technology, Human Values, and Leisure,* ed. Max Kaplan and Philip Bosserman (Nashville: Abingdon, 1971), p. 77.

[12] C. S. Lewis, *Christian Reflections* (Grand Rapids: Eerdmans, 1967), p. 34.

[13] James T. Farrell, *A Note on Literary Criticism* (New York: Vanguard, 1936), pp. 176–77. Another good summary of the values and functions of literature is that by Rosenblatt, *Literature as Exploration,* especially chap. 2.

[14]Matthew Arnold, "The Study of Poetry," in *Criticism: The Major Statements*, ed. Charles Kaplan (New York: St. Martin's Press, 1975), pp. 403–4.

[15]Chad Walsh, "The Advantages of the Christian Faith for a Writer," in *The Christian Imagination: Essays on Literature and the Arts*, ed. Leland Ryken (Grand Rapids: Baker, 1981), p. 308.

[16]Lewis, *Christian Reflections*, p. 10.

[17]Pablo Picasso, *The Arts*, May 1923.

[18]Dorothy Sayers, "Towards a Christian Aesthetic," in *Unpopular Opinions* (London: Victor Gollanz, 1946), p. 37.

[19]Northrop Frye, *The Educated Imagination* (Bloomington: Indiana University Press, 1964), pp. 27–28.

[20]Robert Frost, "Education by Poetry," as reprinted in *The Norton Reader*, 5th ed., ed. Arthur M. Eastman (New York: W. W. Norton, 1980), p. 415.

[21]C. S. Lewis, *An Experiment in Criticism*, pp. 79, 81.

[22]John Crowe Ransom, "Poetry: A Note in Ontology," in *Critiques and Essays in Criticism*, ed. Robert Wooster Stallman (New York: Ronald Press, 1949), p. 40.

[23]Vladimir Nabokov, *Lectures on Literature*, ed. Fredson Bowers (New York: Harcourt Brace Jovanovich, 1980), p. 5.

[24]Andrew Wyeth, as quoted by Virginia Stem Owens, "On Praising God with Our Senses," in *The Christian Imagination*, ed. Ryken, p. 380.

[25]J. R. R. Tolkien, "On Fairy-Stories," in *Essays Presented to Charles Williams*, ed. C. S. Lewis (Grand Rapids: Eerdmans, 1966), p. 75.

[26]Flannery O'Connor, *Mystery and Manners*, ed. Sally and Robert Fitzgerald (New York: Farrar, Straus and Giroux, 1957, 1962), p. 76.

[27]Samuel Johnson, "Preface to Shakespeare," in *Criticism: The Major Statements*, ed. Kaplan, p. 264.

[28]Frye, *The Educated Imagination*, pp. 124–25.

[29]Francis Schaeffer, "Some Perspectives on Art," in *The Christian Imagination*, ed. Ryken, p. 96.

[30]Sayers, *Unpopular Opinions*, p. 37.

[31]H. Richard Niebuhr, *The Responsible Self* (New York: Harper and Row, 1963), pp. 151–52, 161.

[32] James A. Fischer, *How to Read the Bible* (Englewood Cliffs: Prentice-Hall, 1981), p. 43.

[33] John Charles Cooper, *Fantasy and the Human Spirit* (New York: Seabury, 1975), pp. 1–2.

[34] Plato *The Republic*, bk. 10, in *Criticism: The Major Texts*, ed. Walter Jackson Bate (New York: Harcourt, Brace and World, 1952), pp. 46, 49.

[35] Sir Philip Sidney, "An Apology for Poetry," in *Criticism: The Major Statements*, ed. Kaplan, p. 124.

[36] Owen Barfield, *Poetic Diction: A Study in Meaning* (New York: McGraw-Hill, 1964), p. 171.

[37] Charles Williams, *Reason and Beauty in the Poetic Mind* (Oxford: Oxford University Press, 1933), p. 5.

[38] T. S. Eliot, *The Sacred Wood* (London: Methuen, 1920, 1960), preface, p. viii.

[39] W. H. Auden, "Squares and Oblongs," in *Poets at Work* (New York: Harcourt, Brace, 1948), p. 171.

[40] Dylan Thomas, "Poetic Manifesto," in *The Poet's Work*, ed. Reginald Gibbons (Boston: Houghton Mifflin, 1979), pp. 185–86, 190.

[41] Robert Frost, "The Figure a Poem Makes," in *Writers on Writing*, ed. Walter Allen (Boston: The Writer, 1948), p. 22.

[42] Lewis, *An Experiment in Criticism*, pp. 82–83, 91–92.

[43] Robert Frost, as quoted in Elizabeth Drew, *Poetry: A Modern Guide to Its Understanding* (New York: Dell, 1959), p. 84.

[44] Auriel Kolna, "Contrasting the Ethical with the Aesthetical," *British Journal of Aesthetics* 12 (1972): 340.

[45] Alvin Kernan, "The Idea of Literature," *New Literary History* 5 (1973): 35.

[46] I gleaned the details about Hemingway and Thomas from, respectively, Carlos Baker, *Hemingway: The Writer as Artist* (Princeton: Princeton University Press, 1952), p. 97; and John Ackerman, *Dylan Thomas: His Life and Work* (London: Oxford University Press, 1964), pp. 123–24. The quotation from Hopkins comes from "Poetry and Verse," as quoted in *Gerard Manley Hopkins: The Major Poems*, ed. Walford Davies (London: J. M. Dent and Sons, 1979), p. 38.

[47] Lewis, *An Experiment in Criticism*, p. 84.

[48] Blaise Pascal *Pensees* 2.139.

49John Milton, *Of Education*.

50Matthew Arnold, "Literature and Science," in *Prose of the Victorian Period*, ed. William C. Buckley (Boston: Houghton Mifflin, 1958), pp. 493–94.

51Dorothy Sayers, *The Mind of the Maker* (Elnora, N.Y.: Meridian Press, 1956), p. 34.

52Abraham Kuyper, *Lectures on Calvinism* (Grand Rapids: Eerdmans, 1931; reprint 1981), p. 142, see footnote.

53Chad Walsh, "The Advantages of the Christian Faith for a Writer," p. 308.

54H. L. Mencken, as quoted by D. G. Kehl, *Literary Style of the Old Bible and the New* (Indianapolis: Bobbs-Merrill, 1970), p. 7.

55Lewis, *Christian Reflections*, p. 21.

56John Calvin, *Institutes of the Christian Religion*, ed. John T. McNeill (Philadelphia: Westminster, 1960), 1:720.

57Norman Geisler, "The Christian as Pleasure-Seeker," *Christianity Today*, 25 September 1975, p. 11.

58Fyodor Dostoyevsky, *The Brothers Karamazov* (New York: Modern Library, 1950), p. 127; Aldous Huxley, *Brave New World Revisited* (New York: Harper and Row, 1958), p. 52. Huxley goes on to observe that Hitler's rallies "were masterpieces of ritual and theatrical art" and to quote an observer's statement that "for grandiose beauty I have never seen any ballet to compare with the Nuremberg rally."

59Margaret Ho, "Reflecting a God of Beauty," *Eternity*, November 1982, p. 29.

60John Milton, *Apology for Smectymnuus*, in *John Milton: Complete Poems and Major Prose*, ed. Merritt Y. Hughes (New York: Odyssey Press, 1957), p. 693.

61Lewis, *Christian Reflections*, pp. 33–34.

62Frank Gaebelein, "The Christian Use of Leisure," in *A Varied Harvest* (Grand Rapids: Eerdmans, 1967), p. 118.

63Paul Elmen, *The Restoration of Meaning to Contemporary Life* (Garden City: Doubleday, 1958).

64Lewis, *Christian Reflections*, p. 10.

65For further discussion on the fourfold scheme, one can profitably consult chapter 1 of M. H. Abrams's book *The Mirror and the Lamp: Romantic Theory* and the Critical Tradition (Oxford: Oxford University Press, 1953).

66Joyce Cary, Art and Reality (New York: Harper and Brothers, 1958), pp. 105, 116, 137.

67John Shea, Stories of God (Chicago: Thomas More Press, 1978), p. 9.

68David Lodge, Language of Fiction (London: Routledge and Kegan Paul, 1966), p. 65.

69Schaeffer, "Some Perspectives on Art," p. 85.

70Rosenblatt, Literature as Exploration, p. 8.

71This is the last line of Percy B. Shelley's essay A Defence of Poetry.

72For details on Augustine's views on literature, see Confessions 3.2; and The City of God 2.14.

73Sidney's treatise, which I regard as the greatest of all the "classic texts of literary criticism," is entitled An Apology for Poetry (sometimes also entitled A Defence of Poesie). It will repay all the attention that a person gives it and is especially important as a source of Christian literary theory. It is often reprinted, as in Criticism: The Major Statements, ed. Kaplan, pp. 108–47.

74Lewis, "Christianity and Culture," in The Christian Imagination, ed. Ryken, p. 27.

75T. S. Eliot, "Religion and Literature," in The Christian Imagination, ed. Ryken, p. 150.

76Schaeffer, "Some Perspectives on Art," p. 87.

77Malcolm Muggeridge, Jesus Rediscovered (Garden City: Doubleday, 1969), p. 79.

78Percy B. Shelley, "A Defence of Poetry," in Criticism: The Major Statements, ed. Kaplan, p. 364; and William Wordsworth, "Preface to Lyrical Ballads," in the same source, p. 305.

79Jean-Paul Sartre, What is Literature?, trans. Bernard Frechtman (New York: Philosophical Library, 1949), p. 46.

80Ibid.

81Nabokov, "Good Readers and Good Writers," in Lectures on Literature, ed. Bowers, pp. 1, 4.

82Sartre, What Is Literature?, pp. 56, 61.

83Shelley, "A Defence of Poetry," p. 377.

84Robert Frost, "The Figure a Poem Makes," in Writers on Writing, ed. Allen, p. 23.

85Norman Foerster, "The Esthetic Judgment and the Ethical Judgment," in The Intent of the Critic, ed. Donald A. Stauffer (Princeton: Princeton University Press, 1941), pp. 69–70.

[86]O'Connor, *Mystery and Manners*, p. 84.

[87]Emerson, "The Poet," p. 531; Sartre, *What Is Literature?*, p. 45.

[88]Simon O. Lesser, *Fiction and the Unconscious* (Chicago: University of Chicago Press, 1957, 1975), p. 151.

[89]Sayers, *Unpopular Opinions*, pp. 39–40.

[90]Lesser, *Fiction and the Unconscious*, p. 253.

[91]Aldous Huxley, "Tragedy and the Whole Truth," in *Tragedy: Vision and Form*, ed. Robert W. Corrigan (San Francisco: Chandler, 1965), p. 77.

[92]Walker Percy, "Walker Percy, The Man and the Novelist: An Interview," in *The Southern Review*, n.s., 4 (1968): 279.

[93]Stanley Fish, *Surprised by Sin: The Reader in Paradise Lost* (New York: St. Martin's Press, 1967), p. 84.

[94]Lesser, *Fiction and the Unconscious*, p. 253.

[95]Northrop Frye, *The Great Code: The Bible and Literature* (New York: Harcourt Brace Jovanovich, 1982), p. 80.

[96]Wolfgang Iser, "Interaction Between Text and Reader," in *The Reader in the Text: Essays on Audience and Interpretation*, ed. Susan R. Suleiman and Inge Crosman (Princeton: Princeton University Press, 1980), p. 110.

[97]Vincent Buckley, *Poetry and Morality* (London: Chatto and Windus, 1959), pp. 217, 225.

[98]Louise M. Rosenblatt, *The Reader, the Text, the Poem: The Transactional Theory of the Literary Work* (Carbondale: Southern Illinois University Press, 1978), pp. 144, 165.

[99]Richard E. Palmer, *Hermeneutics: Interpretation Theory in Schleiermacher, Dilthey, Heidegger, and Gadamer* (Evanston: Northwestern University Press, 1969), p. 182.

[100]David Bleich, *Readings and Feelings: An Introduction to Subjective Criticism* (Urbana: National Council of Teachers of English, 1975), pp. 3–4.

[101]Paul Ricoeur, *The Conflict of Interpretations: Essays in Hermeneutics* (Evanston: Northwestern University Press, 1974), p. 3.

[102]S. L. Bethell, *Essays on Literary Criticism and the English Tradition* (London: Dennis Dobson, 1948), pp. 24–25.

[103]Lewis, *An Experiment in Criticism*, pp. 138–40.

[104]Ibid., p. 19.

[105] Jonathan Culler, *Structuralist Poetics: Structuralism, Linguistics, and the Study of Literature* (Ithaca: Cornell University Press, 1975), p. 115.

[106] Rosenblatt, *Literature as Exploration*, p. 8.

[107] William Faulkner's Nobel acceptance speech is reprinted in *Six Great Modern Short Novels* (New York: Dell, 1954), pp. 324–26.

[108] Cary, *Art and Reality*, p. 114.

[109] Baudelaire, as quoted by J. Middleton Murry, *The Problem of Style* (London: Oxford University Press, 1922), p. 30.

[110] Ralph W. Rader, "The Concept of Genre and Eighteenth-Century Studies," in *New Approaches to Eighteenth-Century Literature*, ed. Phillip Harth (New York: Columbia University Press, 1974), pp. 79–115.

[111] Sigmund Freud, *New Introductory Lectures on Psycho-Analysis*, trans. W. J. H. Sprott (New York: W. W. Norton, 1933), p. 216.

[112] James Sire, *How to Read Slowly* (Downers Grove: InterVarsity Press, 1978), pp. 14–15.

[113] Alvin Toffler, *Future Shock* (New York: Random House, 1970), p. 139.

[114] Clifford Geertz, "Ritual and Social Change: A Javanese Example," *American Anthropologist* 59 (1957): 33.

[115] Nathan A. Scott, "The Modern Experiment in Criticism: A Theological Appraisal," in *The New Orpheus: Essays Toward a Christian Poetic*, ed. Nathan A. Scott (New York: Sheed and Ward, 1964), pp. 156–63.

[116] Boris Uspensky, *A Poetics of Composition*, trans. V. Zavarin and S. Wittig (Berkeley: University of California Press, 1973), p. 137.

[117] O'Connor, *Mystery and Manners*, p. 75.

[118] Richard Stevens and Thomas J. Musial, *Reading, Discussing, and Writing about the Great Books* (Boston: Houghton Mifflin, 1970), p. 24.

[119] T. S. Eliot, *The Use of Poetry and the Use of Criticism* (Cambridge, Mass.: Harvard University Press, 1933), p. 147.

[120] Sheldon Sacks, *Fiction and the Shape of Belief* (Berkeley: University of California Press, 1964), p. 251.

[121] C. S. Lewis, *English Literature in the Sixteenth Century* (Oxford: Oxford University Press, 1954), p. 331.

[122]The quotation is from T. S. Eliot's great essay "Religion and Literature," which is a classic that needs to be read and pondered by anyone wishing to integrate literature and Christianity. I have quoted from the essay as reprinted in *The Christian Imagination*, ed. Ryken, pp. 142, 153.

[123]Oscar Wilde, "Preface to *The Picture of Dorian Gray*," printed in 1891; quoted from *The Norton Anthology of English Literature*, 4th ed., ed. M. H. Abrams (New York: W. W. Norton, 1979), 2:1682.

[124]Plato's comments occur chiefly in *The Republic*, bk. 10.

[125]Aristotle *The Poetics*, chap. 13.

[126]For Sidney's comments, see his treatise *An Apology for Poetry*, which also bears the title *A Defence of Poesie*.

[127]Wordsworth, "Preface to *Lyrical Ballads*."

[128]Arnold, *Essay on Wordsworth*.

[129]Ernest Hemingway, *Death in the Afternoon* (New York: Charles Scribner's Sons, 1932), p. 4.

[130]Rosenblatt, *Literature as Exploration*, pp. 16, 18.

[131]Philip Hobsbaum, *A Theory of Communication* (London: Macmillan, 1970), pp. 143, 162.

[132]Keith F. McKean, *The Moral Measure of Literature* (Westport, Conn.: Greenwood Press, 1961), pp. 11–12.

[133]Wordsworth, "Preface to *Lyrical Ballads*," in *Criticism: The Major Statements*, ed. Kaplan, pp. 305–6.

[134]Coleridge, *Shakespearean Criticism*, ed. Thomas Middleton Raysor (London: J. M. Dent and Sons, 1960), 2:92.

[135]Eliot, "Religion and Literature," in *The Christian Imagination*, ed. Ryken, p. 150.

[136]Elder Olson, "An Outline of Poetic Theory," in *Critics and Criticism*, ed. Ronald S. Crane (Chicago: University of Chicago Press, 1952), p. 566.

[137]Plato *The Republic*, bk. 10, in *Criticism: The Major Statements*, ed. Kaplan, p. 14.

[138]Quoted in *Novelists on the Novel*, ed. Miriam Allott (London: Routledge and Kegan Paul, 1959), p. 89.

[139]"The Junk-Food Murder," *Newsweek*, 20 September 1982, p. 34.

[140]*Reader's Digest*, January 1983, pp. 49–53.

141 Daniel M. Stashower, "On First Looking into Chapman's Holden: Speculations on a Murder," *The American Scholar,* Summer 1983, pp. 373–77.

142 Sidney, "Apology for Poetry," in *Criticism: The Major Statements,* ed. Kaplan, p. 123.

143 Ibid., p. 134.

144 Alexander Pope, *An Essay on Man,* Epistle 2, lines 217–20.

145 Sacks, *Fiction and the Shape of Belief,* p. 254. Sacks further says that it is impossible to determine "the moral effect of a novel . . . by some of its parts."

146 T. S. Eliot, "Religion and Literature," p. 147.

147 Sacks, *Fiction and the Shape of Belief,* pp. 249–50.

148 I am indebted for this concise definition to Harry Blamires, *The Christian Mind* (London: S.P.C.K., 1966), p. 98.

149 The phrase comes from Tolkien, "On Fairy-Stories," p. 79.

150 Blamires, *Christian Mind,* p. 98.

151 Calvin Seerveld, *A Christian Critique of Art* (St. Catharines, Ontario: Association for Reformed Scientific Studies, 1963), p. 52.

152 Blamires, *Christian Mind,* p. 45.

153 Coleridge, *Shakespearean Criticism,* 2:30.

154 The example is cited by Wayne C. Booth, *The Rhetoric of Fiction* (Chicago: University of Chicago Press, 1961), p. 389.

155 *Boccaccio on Poetry,* trans. and ed. Charles G. Osgood (New York: Liberal Arts Press, 1956), p. 74.

156 Plato *The Republic,* bk. 10, in *Criticism: The Major Statements,* ed. Kaplan, p. 16.

157 T. S. Eliot, "Religion and Literature," pp. 148, 150.

158 Coleridge, *Shakespearean Criticism,* 2:92–93.

159 Lewis, *Christian Reflections,* p. 10.

For Further Reading

Baxter, Kay M. **Contemporary Theatre and the Christian Faith.** Nashville: Abingdon, 1964. Van Zanten, John. **Caught in the Act: Modern Drama as Prelude to the Gospel.** Philadelphia: Westminster, 1971.

Both books show that modern drama, though it does not affirm a Christian world view, explores the religious issues to which the Christian faith speaks. Both books are out of print.

Cary, Norman R. **Christian Criticism in the Twentieth Century.** Port Washington, N.Y.: Kennikat Press, 1975.

A reference guide to some common theological approaches to literature.

Christianity and Literature, a journal published quarterly by the Conference on Christianity and Literature.

This is the best source for keeping abreast of what is happening in the field of religion and literature. Each issue includes book reviews and an annotated bibliography of books and articles that have dealt with topics of interest to Christian critics. Current mailing address: Department of English, Baylor University, Waco, TX 76798.

Eliot, T. S. **"Religion and Literature,"** in *Selected Essays.* New York: Harcourt, Brace and World, 1932.

The most important single essay on the subject. Reprinted in The Christian Imagination, *ed. Leland Ryken.*

Frye, Roland M. **Perspective on Man: Literature and the Christian Tradition.** Philadelphia: Westminster, 1961.

Especially valuable for the middle section, which explores how literature "furnishes insight into human life and increases the value of that life by the nurture of beauty, of understanding, and of compassion" and how literature probes "the ultimate dilemmas of the human soul." Out of print.

Lewis, C. S. **An Experiment in Criticism.** Cambridge: Cambridge University Press, 1965.

The book does not directly relate literature to Christianity, but it is the most complete statement of literary theory by an influential Christian writer and thinker.

O'Connor, Flannery. **Mystery and Manners.** Ed. Sally and Robert Fitzgerald. New York: Farrar, Straus and Giroux, 1957.

A collection of essays and addresses by a leading Christian writer of fiction. A goldmine of insights.

Ryken, Leland, ed. **The Christian Imagination: Essays on Literature and the Arts.** Grand Rapids: Baker, 1981.

A collection of thirty-nine essays by thirty-one authors, this anthology covers the whole range of topics related to integrating biblical Christianity and the arts.

_____. **Triumphs of the Imagination: Literature in Christian Perspective.** Downers Grove: InterVarsity, 1979.

Attempts to provide a biblical basis for reading and studying literature, and to illustrate those principles with explications of literary works. Out of print.

Scott, Nathan A., Jr., ed. **The Climate of Faith in Modern Literature.** New York: Seabury, 1964.

A collection of essays by various experts in modern literature. Out of print.

_____. **The New Orpheus: Essays Toward a Christian Poetic.** New York: Sheed and Ward, 1964.

Twenty-one essays by various Christian scholars. The best thinking of an earlier generation of literary theorists as they attempted to formulate a Christian philosophy of literature. Out of print.

Tennyson, G. B., and Ericson, Edward R., Jr., eds. **Religion and Modern Literature: Essays in Theory and Criticism.** Grand Rapids: Eerdmans, 1975.

Theoretic essays on how to integrate literature and Christianity, followed by critical essays on modern literature from a religious perspective. Out of print.

Veith, Gene Edward, Jr. **The Gift of Art: The Place of the Arts in Scripture.** Downers Grove: InterVarsity, 1983.

Concerned mainly with the visual arts, this book is a treasure of biblical principles that apply to all the arts, including literature.

Index

191